The Manna God:
40 Days in Exodus

Nancy Hulshult

The Manna God: 40 Days in Exodus

©2023 Created by Nancy Hulshult. All rights reserved.

ISBN: 979-8-9856988-3-1

Published by:
NarratusCreative | Narratus Press
P.O. Box 1413
Hamilton, OH 45012

Layout/Design: NarratusCreative | narratuscreative.com
Cover Photo Credits: Greg Schanding

Produced in the United States of America

Foreword

As a pastor of 20+ years, I have been afforded the opportunity to teach and preach on a variety of Biblical topics, perhaps none more rich in the imagery of God's deliverance than the record of the Israelite exodus.

While all Scripture is God-breathed and useful for teaching (see 2 Timothy 3:16), the Biblical accent of the record of the Exodus rings true in the hearts of believers world-wide because of the obvious parallel to our everyday 21st century lives.

Who among us hasn't cried out to God in the midst of bondage and slavery to sin? Who among us hasn't been delivered by God and then quickly reverted back to a lifestyle of complaining and a longing for "life back in Egypt"? Who among us hasn't been guilty of forgetting about the faithfulness of God? The stubbornness and forgetfulness of the Israelite people is but just one facet of the whole picture of the Exodus.

What *The Manna God: 40 Days in Exodus* offers the reader is a chance to more fully step inside the Exodus account. Perhaps over the next 40 days of this journey...

- You'll begin to more closely identify with Moses' mother and the courage she mustered to protect her child from certain death.

- You'll come to identify with Moses and his role as deliverer and mouthpiece of God. Maybe like Moses, you've developed a long list of reason why "I just can't serve because...".

- You'll have an opportunity to reflect on your own burning bush interactions with God. How do you measure up when compared to Moses' response?

- You'll have an opportunity to reflect on the promises of God. Do you really believe in them, or are they just words on the pages of your Bible?

• You'll reflect on the stories you'll tell your children and your grandchildren. Will they be tales of the faithfulness of God or of your wanderings in the wilderness?

• You'll come to understand the new rhythms and seasons God created for the Israelite people. What will serve as the spiritual markers in your journey with God?

• You'll begin to question how you're using your talents and abilities for Kingdom purposes.

• You'll consider what "golden calves" you may have created in your own life.

Perhaps the greatest lesson you'll learn over these next 40 days is the truth that God will stop at nothing to see His children come into right relationship with Himself. What the Exodus was really all about was deliverance, not just of the Israelite people, but deliverance for all mankind through the Son of God, Jesus Christ.

It has become obvious to me from having known Nancy for many years that her heart mirrors the heart of God: to see people delivered from bondage and to begin walking in the fullness and freedom that only Christ offers.

Through Nancy's devotional writings, scriptural analysis and reflective questions, *The Manna God: 40 Days in Exodus* offers you an opportunity to dive into Exodus at a level where few would venture.

Let me encourage you to take this journey. Put yourself in the shoes of Jochebed, Moses, Aaron, Pharaoh, Jethro, Zipporah, the priests, the Israelite people, Bezalel. Create space and time over these next 40 days to allow God to speak clearly and directly to your heart. Be encouraged, and keep moving forward.

Andy Hoover
Pastor Andy Hoover
Lead Pastor - Dayspring Church
Author of *31 Days Towards Practical Living*

Dedication & Appreciation

To my husband and best friend for life, Darrell Hulshult.

To our next generation, especially our grandchildren, who fill our lives with love and laughter: Evan, Reese, Madelyn, Andrew, Remy, Alex, Conner, Joey, Seth, Nathan, Bennett, Asher, Aaron, Junie, Noah.

To my spiritual mentors, who ground me in truth, faith, and love: Pastor Felix R. Escobar, and Dr. Michael E. Dantley.

To my editors:
Debbie Day, Mary Lou Hudek, and Chad Shepherd.

To my friend, Greg Schanding,
for permitting to use his beautiful photographs for the book cover.

To my friend, Francesca King,
for giving me the nudge to write a second devotional.

To contributors from the 2022 Dayspring Women's Retreat:

Cindy Speakman

Kamille Dawkins Dungan

Stacie L. Johnson

Jessica Hulshult

Annetta Weimer

Format and Design: Denise Chaney of NarratusCreative

Photos by Greg Schanding. Front cover photo: "Crossing the Cowlick", Back cover photo: "Sunset on Silver Lake".

Other books by Nancy Hulshult:
I'm Still Here, Aún Sigo Aquí (Spanish edition), *Imagine You, Imaginárte a Ti* (Spanish edition), *God's Restorative Nature*

Table of Contents

Foreword... i
Dedication & Appreciation............. iii
Introduction.. vii

Day 1, Chapter One......................... 1

Day 2, Chapter Two 7

Day 3, Chapter Three 15

Day 4, Chapter Four 21

Day 5, Chapter Five......................... 29

Day 6, Chapter Six 35

Day 7, Chapter Seven 41

Day 8, Chapter Eight 49

Day 9, Chapter Nine........................ 59

Day 10, Chapter Ten........................ 67

Day 11, Chapter Eleven.................. 73

Day 12, Chapter Twelve 77

Day 13, Chapter Thirteen.............. 87

Day 14, Chapter Fourteen 93

Day 15, Chapter Fifteen 103

Day 16, Chapter Sixteen................ 103

Day 17, Chapter Seventeen........... 109

Day 18, Chapter Eighteen.............. 113

Day 19, Chapter Nineteen 117

Day 20, Chapter Twenty................ 123

Day 21, Chapter Twenty-One 127

Day 22, Chapter Twenty-Two.......... 131

Day 23, Chapter Twenty-Three..... 135

Day 24, Chapter Twenty-Four....... 139

Day 25, Chapter Twenty-Five 143

Day 26, Chapter Twenty-Six.......... 151

Day 27, Chapter Twenty-Seven.... 155

Day 28, Chapter Twenty-Eight...... 159

Day 29, Chapter Twenty-Nine 163

Day 30, Chapter Thirty 167

Day 31, Chapter Thirty-One.......... 171

Day 32, Chapter Thirty-Two 181

Day 33, Chapter Thirty-Three 187

Day 34, Chapter Thirty-Four 189

Day 35, Chapter Thirty-Five 199

Day 36, Chapter Thirty-Six............. 203

Day 37, Chapter Thirty-Seven....... 207

Day 38, Chapter Thirty-Eight 211

Day 39, Chapter Thirty-Nine......... 215

Day 40, Chapter Forty 219

Conclusion 233

Notes.. 237

Afterword.. 245

Appendix 251

Testimonies...................................... 269

Introduction

Have you ever been disappointed in yourself? In other people? So has God...all the time. He appoints us to be his people; in return, we disappoint him on a regular basis, yet he forgives and loves us. He wants more for us, so he always gives us another chance to keep our appointment. Don't believe me? Read Exodus. Our God never gives up on us. Never.

Exodus is a story in the Bible about God, his people,and their escape from captivity to the Promised Land. The Hebrew word for Exodus is "departure from Egypt." The Greek word for Exodus is "the road out". Their story is our story, if you are a Bible believer. Our story is so significant that the Lord told Moses to write it down for all generations to remember. Here are three verses that speak to God being the author of Exodus history with Moses as his recorder.

> *Exodus 17:14: Then the Lord said to Moses, "Write this on a scroll as something to be remembered and make sure that Joshua hears it, because I will completely blot out the name of Amalek from under heaven."*

> *Exodus 24:4: Moses then wrote down everything the Lord had said. He got up early the next morning and built an altar at the foot of the mountain and set up twelve stone pillars representing the twelve tribes of Israel.*

> *Exodus 34:27-28: 27 Then the Lord said to Moses, "Write down these words, for in accordance with these words I have made a covenant with you and with Israel." 28 Moses was there with the Lord forty days and forty nights without eating bread or drinking water. And he wrote on the tablets the words of the covenant—the Ten Commandments.*

The first verses of the book of Exodus begin with the names of the 12 sons or tribes of Israel, the sons of Jacob. With Joseph already in

Egypt, the other 11 sons joined him: Reuben, Simeon, Levi, Judah; Issachar, Zebulun, Benjamin; Dan, Naphtali; Gad and Asher. These are the family names of the chosen people of God, called the Israelites. To best appreciate their journey from sonship to slavery to the Promised Land, imagine yourself as a member of one of these tribes. For fun, pick one and be a part of the family as they travel to Egypt, out of Egypt to the desert wilderness, and on to the Promised Land of Canaan. Let's picture ourselves on the journey and what it would be like to be forced into slavery to make bricks for the king; to suffer through some plagues and to be exonerated from others; to prepare our escape from the powerful Pharaoh; to cook the Passover meal and spread lamb's blood on our doorposts to save our firstborn sons; to watch the pursuing chariots in fear; to pass through the sea on dry land in victory; to watch dead Egyptian soldiers and horses wash up on the shore; to survive 40 years in the desert with blessings of food from the sky and punishments for our lack of faith as a people; and finally to arrive at the Promised Land.

I feel tired and weary just thinking of the family's journey. I am impressed that, although weary of their complaints and betrayals, God stayed faithful and present with them "through all their journeys", as the last verse in Exodus says. Verse 40:38, reads: *For the cloud of the Lord was upon the tabernacle by day, and fire was on it by night, in the sight of all the house of Israel, throughout all their journeys.*

Imagine traveling and seeing the day cloud and the night fire, knowing that God is always with us. Imagine being in the desert wilderness with nothing to feed us or our family, but knowing that we could sleep at night because our Manna God would send sustenance from the heavens, except on the Sabbath. Imagine the man of God, Moses, chosen to lead us with his doubts, temper, his speech impediments, yet with his incredibly intimate relationship with God. Imagine being in the family of Israel and seeing all the miracles and adventures from Egypt to the Promised Land. Are we going to make it out alive?

Now choose your family and we will read our family's history together for the next 40 days and walk with them through the 40 chapters of the Exodus.

I chose the family of Levi for two reasons: (1) Moses was from the tribe of Levi, and I wanted to live vicariously through his challenges as the reluctant leader with unrelenting doubts, physical flaws, and the temper that comes with dealing with stubborn, complaining people; and (2) my maternal grandfather's name is Levenson. "Levi" is a shortened name for one of my favorite relatives. Gordon Elias Levenson, my uncle, has had a profound influence on my life. His obituary is a poetic tribute to the man and family legend:

"On the night of September 10th, 2008, early in the pre-dawn hours, Gordon Elias Levenson had a dream. He dreamed of a perfect world where everyone is polite and stops to help a neighbor. His dream was of a world where people listened to each other and showed respect to their fellow man. A world free of conflict and war, free of poverty and suffering, and free of sickness and debilitating disease. He dreamed of the perpetual bottomless cup of coffee in a white porcelain Navy mug sitting in a worn and comfortable chair, with just the right padding conformed over the years to perfectly fit his posture. He dreamed of sitting at a table surrounded by all his friends and neighbors who stopped by, searching for the warmth of friendship and the words of a wise listener. His presence was warmer than any wood-burning Buffalo stove could ever give off. He dreamed of his wife of 49 years, Vera, sitting by his side, having just finished a batch of strawberry jam and a cherry pie. While sitting in his kitchen, with his coffee, his dream produces a call from his sons and daughter. A call from Thailand, with his son Burt, telling about his latest adventure in Asia. A call from his sons Mark and Tim comes over an Alaskan ship radio with a total of the latest Halibut catch. A call from daughter Rebecca, from the Ann Arbor Art Fair, relaying the day's sales report of her business and the news of the day. In his dream he remembers with pride the 30 years of teaching Ann Arbor students and how he helped to shape the thinking and ethics in a Michigan town. He dreams of walking down Main Street where bankers, lawyers, policemen, politicians, doctors, and shoppers see him and yell out, "Hi Gordy!". In his dream, the

birds are fed, the grass is mowed, flowers are in bloom, and he is watching with glee as a bold squirrel is still trying to outwit his latest obstacle to the bird feeder. Gordy Levenson is now living that dream. Gordon Levenson was born on February 28th, 1927 in Hamilton, OH. He married Vera Ziepfel in 1950. His wife and three sisters, Edith, Mary, and Peg, preceded him in death. He is survived by two sisters; JoAnn (Dick) Meyer and Becky (Jack) Eggleton, daughter, Rebecca (Karl Dyke) sons, Burt (Amanda), Mark (Joan) and Tim. He is also survived by four wonderful grandchildren, Malisa, Gregg, Eli, and Isaac, and many more relatives and friends, too numerous to list. Gordy taught school in the Ann Arbor School District for over 30 years. He was a graduate of the University of Michigan where he was a nationally ranked gymnast. He completed his Masters degree from Michigan State University. He was a naval veteran having served in WWII. He was a long time member of Old St. Patrick's Catholic Church."

From our annual trips to see Uncle Gordy and Aunt Vera for Thanksgiving, I can see how I have developed a love for nature, gymnastics, adventure, conversation, travel, the love of my home town, and the power of friendship and community.

Take a minute or two to write your thoughts about your influential relatives or friends who have been a part of your life journey. What positive traits do you take from them that show through your life? What positive traits about yourself would you want to pass on to your next generation? Then let's go back to the days of our corporate family history and see how much we can relate to the life journey of the sons of Israel.

DAY**1**

Exodus
Chapter One

Summary:

The sons of Israel (Jacob) moved to Egypt with their brother, Joseph: Ruben, Simeon, Levi, Judah, Issachar, Zebulun, Benjamin, Dan, Naphtali, Gad, and Asher. Seventy descendants were already in Egypt.

What caused the Israelites to be oppressed into slavery?

> *Verses 6-7: "Now Joseph and all his brothers and all that generation died, but the Israelites were exceedingly fruitful; they multiplied greatly, increased in numbers and became so numerous that the land was filled with them."*

Their population grew to numbers that caused the king to fear an imbalance of power or disloyalty to his throne. He feared that they would become more powerful than the Egyptians. In today's world of politics, leaders and analysts consider the demographics of the United States to predict outcomes of national, regional, and local elections. With growing numbers of immigrants and refugees from other countries, soon the white majority may become a minority. That makes some leaders very nervous about their current political power. Ancient Egypt was not a democracy that relied on votes by the people, but Pharaoh watched the numbers of Israelites growing and saw the potential for them to wage war against Egypt and/or to leave the country, thus depriving Egypt of its forced manual labor.

Consider the Civil War in the United States in light of the balance of power and economics. Powerful white plantation owners enslaved black people for the manual labor needed to produce crops in both the North and the South. The war was fought by some to free the slaves based upon human rights and the dignity of each person, but it was fought by others to maintain the current agricultural economy and the wealth of the plantation owners. As the numbers of freed slaves grew after the war, one can imagine the thoughts of those in political and economic power to be similar to those of Pharaoh.

Verses 8-10: "Then a new king, to whom Joseph meant nothing, came to power in Egypt. 'Look,' he said to his people, "the Israelites have become far too numerous for us. 10 Come, we must deal shrewdly with them or they will become even more numerous and, if war breaks out, will join our enemies, fight against us and leave the country."

The king had no knowledge or history of their brother, Joseph, whose deeds had helped Egypt to escape famine. His unfounded suspicions and fear speak to the need for leaders to rely on past history for current wisdom. To compare it to the national leaders of today in the United States, when a presidential election results in a new leader of a different political party, the new policies and laws are supported or created by one who generally disagrees with most of what the former leader had supported. It seems as though the former president and political party mean nothing to the new president and leaders in power.

With Joseph's power and influence diminishing with the new Egyptian king, the Israelites' political status diminished as well. However, the Israelites were a hardy people, who thrived even in oppression. Ironically, the king's attempt to suppress and keep them in his country ultimately resulted in their escape from Egypt, with God's help and a lot of insufferable plagues, of course.

Verses 12-14: "But the more they were oppressed, the more they multiplied and spread; so the Egyptians came to dread the Israelites and worked them ruthlessly. They made their lives bitter with harsh labor in brick and mortar and with all kinds of work in the fields; in all their harsh labor the Egyptians worked them ruthlessly."

What were the results of these perceived threats of numbers, power, suspicion, and disloyalty?

1. Brutal slave drivers wore the Israelites down with crushing labor demands.

2. The more the Egyptians oppressed the Israelites, the more the Israelites multiplied and spread.

3. A raised level of fear led to the king's order to kill all baby boys born to the Israelites.

4. Hebrew midwives refused to obey because they feared God more than the king. They lied to the king about not getting to the babies in time.

> *Verse 17: "The midwives, however, feared God and did not do what the king of Egypt had told them to do; they let the boys live."*

1. God was good to the midwives and their families.
2. Israelites continued to multiply.
3. Israelites became more powerful.
4. This cycle of fear by the Egyptians caused increased oppression toward the Israelites, which resulted in the Israelites becoming even more powerful.
5. The Egyptians feared men. The Israelites and midwives feared God.

> *Verses 20-21: "So God was kind to the midwives and the people increased and became even more numerous. And because the midwives feared God, he gave them families of their own."*

Pharaoh ordered ALL people (not just midwives) to throw all the newborn Hebrew boys into the Nile, which led to Moses being brought into the palace, the exact opposite of Pharaoh's intentions. In a similar situation when Joseph had been thrown into a pit to die from the evil intent of his brothers, Joseph became a powerful leader in Egypt. Joseph voiced his thoughts about God's grand design for his people in Genesis 50:20 You intended to harm me, but God intended it for good to accomplish what is now being done, the saving of many lives.

Reflection:

1. Pharaoh's desire for evil led to good. Because Pharaoh wanted to maintain power, he ordered the death of all male babies. Because Moses was hidden in the Nile River, he was preserved and allowed to live in the palace with the rights and privileges as a Prince of Egypt, which ultimately led to the demise of Pharaoh. When in my life has God turned what was evil into good for the benefit of me and my family?

2. In what ways do I fear man more than I fear God?

3. What is the difference in my motivations to please God vs. my motivations to please man?

Additional Thoughts:

Natalie Custer: The Israelites were powerful but not empowered. God placed Moses to grow up in Egyptian culture to know their ways to be able to deal with Pharaoh and to have some rights and influence as a former Egyptian prince. We fear what we don't know.

Debbie Day: God is always setting up events and details in our lives and in the world for the "big picture". Joseph being sold to the Egyptians resulted in God's glory in the deliverance of the Israelites through Moses. We are in fear of the daily small things that might hurt or inconvenience us because we do not see the big picture.

Response:

_____

_____

_____

_____

DAY**2**

Exodus
Chapter Two

Summary:

*Verse 1: Now a man of the tribe of Levi married a Levite woman, 2 and she became pregnant and gave birth to a son. When **she saw** that he was a fine child, she hid him for three months.3 But when she could hide him no longer, she got a papyrus basket for him and coated it with tar and pitch. Then she placed the child in it and put it among the reeds along the bank of the Nile.*

*Verse 4: His sister stood at a distance **to see** what would happen to him.*

*Verse 5-6: 5 Then Pharaoh's daughter went down to the Nile to bathe, and her attendants were walking along the riverbank. **She saw** the basket among the reeds and sent her female slave to get it. 6 She opened it and **saw** the baby. He was crying, and she felt sorry for him. "This is one of the Hebrew babies," she said.*

Verse 7: Then <u>his sister</u> asked <u>Pharaoh's daughter</u>, "Shall I go and get one of the Hebrew women to nurse the baby for you?"

Verse 8-9: 8 "Yes, go," she answered. So <u>the girl</u> went and got the baby's mother. 9 <u>Pharaoh's daughter</u> said to her, "Take this baby and nurse him for me, and I will pay you." So the woman took the baby and nursed him.

Verse 10: When the child grew older, she took him to Pharaoh's daughter and he became her son. She named him Moses, saying, "I drew him out of the water."

The redemption story of the Exodus, where the Israelites were freed from slavery and delivered out of Egypt, began with the redemption of their leader, Moses. In this poignant story of saving a baby from death or drowning in the Nile, women of all walks of life served as the redeemers or saviors of baby Moses.

First, Moses' Levite mother gave birth to him, hid him for three months, and made a basket to place him in the reeds of the Nile. Second, Moses' big sister (Miriam) watched over him. Third, Pharaoh's daughter, the princess, saw the basket and sent her female slaves to get it. Fourth, courageously, Miriam approached the Pharaoh's daughter, the princess, to suggest a nurse maid for the baby, which was Moses' and Miriam's mother. Fifth, Pharaoh's daughter adopted Moses, knowing full well that the baby should have been killed, according to her father's commands. By adopting Moses, she empowered him to be a prince of Egypt.

More than five women, from the princess to the slave, contributed to the saving of Moses. Because of their **seeing** something special in baby Moses and taking steps to place him in a position to survive and thrive, they helped to produce a powerful leader of Egypt and of Israel. Though some may consider the Bible to be an androcentric story of salvation, I see many examples of women contributing to the redemption of God's people. (See the redemptive role of Moses' wife, Zipporah, in chapter 4.)

> *Verse 11: One day, after Moses had grown up, he went out to where his own people were and watched them at their hard labor. **He saw** an Egyptian beating a Hebrew, one of his own people.*

Moses maintained his identity as a Hebrew, even in the palace with the position of an Egyptian prince. When God creates us, we enter the world in a family structure with a legacy of physical, spiritual, and emotional characteristics that define us and roots us in our culture. As we mature, we take steps to accept or reject components of our roots, which then defines how we live out our adult lives. In the case of Moses, he was able to maintain his role as Egyptian prince until he saw one of his own people suffering.

Moses must have been taught and reminded that he was a Hebrew, nursed and raised by his Hebrew mother for his first years of life. This reminds me of Proverbs 22:6 Train up a child in the way he should go: and when he is old, he will not depart from it.

Verse 12: Looking this way and that and seeing no one, he killed the Egyptian and hid him in the sand.

Moses had time to think about his actions if he had time to look around to see if anyone saw him. He could have reported the violence and beatings to Pharaoh, perhaps pleading for justice or mercy. However, as the adopted Egyptian prince, he was grafted into this system that accepted forced slavery and violent treatment of the Hebrews. This was a defining moment in his life. He had to choose between his own people and his adopted family. He had to choose between peace and mercy or violence and injustice. Moses' action of killing the Egyptian altered the course of the rest of his life. From there he would run to the wilderness to escape. He would go from serving Pharaoh to serving God, from Egyptian idol worship to Hebrew worship of the one, true God of his people. Everything that happened to Moses was to prepare him for his role later to lead the Children of Israel to the Promised Land.

Verse 13: The next day he went out and saw two Hebrews fighting. He asked the one in the wrong, "Why are you hitting your fellow Hebrew?"

As Moses saw fellow Hebrews fighting, he questioned the reason for violence within the family.

Moses' eyes must have been opened to the reality of his life situation. Egyptians were beating Hebrews. Hebrews were fighting Hebrews. Perhaps he did not experience any of this as he was growing up within the walls of the palace. Out in the adult world, he was finding that his privileged life was quite different from the life in the fields and the brick and mortar labor camps of his home country of Egypt.

Verse 14: The man said, "Who made you ruler and judge over us? Are you thinking of killing me as you killed the Egyptian?"

Then Moses was afraid and thought, "What I did must have become known."

Moses was rejected by his people, the Hebrews, who challenged his authority over them. He was also fearful of the Egyptians, since he murdered one and tried to hide it. At this point in his life, he was not aligned with Israel or Egypt. He was a man between cultures, belonging to neither because of his actions. Fear of death motivated Moses to flee, where he landed in Midian to become part of yet another family.

Verse 15: When Pharaoh heard of this, he tried to kill Moses, but Moses fled from Pharaoh and went to live in Midian, where he sat down by a well. Now a priest of Midian had seven daughters, and they came to draw water and fill the troughs to water their father's flock. 17 Some shepherds came along and drove them away, but Moses got up and came to their rescue and watered their flock.

By watering the women's flocks at the well, Moses found favor with the priest of Midian. Moses served as the shepherdesses' rescuer and was invited to their home.

(Wells served as places of divine appointments in the Bible. In Genesis 16, Hagar met an angel at the well of Beer Lahai Roi to learn that she would give Abram a son named Ishmael. In Genesis 29, Jacob fell in love with Rachel at the well and watered her flocks. In John 4, Jesus sat on Jacob's well when he met the Samaritan woman and revealed himself as Messiah. In Moses' case, he finally found rest and a future for himself when he stopped fleeing from Egypt and stopped to rest at the well.)

Verse 21-22: 21 Moses agreed to stay with the man, who gave his daughter Zipporah to Moses in marriage. 22 Zipporah gave birth to a son, and Moses named him Gershom, saying, "I have become a foreigner in a foreign land."

Moses declared his identity in Midian as a foreigner in a foreign land. His adoptive father king died; his native family cried to God for help, and God heard. Soon God would see the people of Israel and would call Moses back to rescue them, to be their savior.

> *Verse 23-25: 23 During that long period, the king of Egypt died. The Israelites groaned in their slavery and cried out, and their cry for help because of their slavery went up to God. 24 God heard their groaning and he remembered his covenant with Abraham, with Isaac and with Jacob. 25 So God looked on the Israelites and was concerned about them.*

The action of hiding in this story is used for the protection of Moses until he can lead the Israelites to the Promised Land and to fulfill God's covenant with his people. As a Hebrew baby, he was hidden in a basket in the Nile River. As an Egyptian prince committing murder, he looked around to make sure no one was watching and he hid his victim in the sand.

After he killed a man, he rescued the shepherd girls. The action of redemption in this story is used to save Moses, and again to save the shepherd girls, and ultimately to save Moses' people. The first redemption was of baby Moses by the Egyptian princess; the second redemption was of the Midian shepherd girls by the murderer Moses; and the third redemption was Moses' acceptance into the shepherd girls' family and then becoming a part of their family.

Reflection:

1. How does this story place emphasis on seeing and being seen or noticed? Consider the birth of Moses, the awakening of Moses as an adult, the rescue of the shepherdesses, and God looking on the Israelites.

2. Is our destiny determined by those who see us or hear us? How important is it to notice others and their conditions? To see and to be seen?

3. How important are the roles of the women in this redemption

story: the midwives, the queen, the princess, Moses' mother, Moses' sister Miriam, the shepherd girls? How might the redemptive story of Moses be different without the actions of each woman in Moses' life?

4. What women have been important in my life? Why?

5. How was the princess received by the royal family when she adopted Moses as her own son? How was Moses treated as an adopted child given the title of prince of the palace?

6. What motivated Moses to take justice into his own hands when he killed the man?

7. Why was violence justified for killing male babies but not justified in defending the Hebrew slave?

8. What have I hidden in my life that needs to come to light?

9. Have I been redeemed from my past sins? Who, besides Jesus, was instrumental in the process of my redemption?

10. How can I advance the process of redemption in someone else's life?

11. As I think about a leader in my life, do I also see those who support him/her? Do I appreciate their supportive roles in order for the leader to be effective?

12. How do I know that God sees me? What evidence do I have that God hears my cries and looks after me?

Response:

_____

_____

_____

DAY**3**

Exodus
Chapter Three

Summary:

Verse 4: "When the Lord saw that he had gone over to look, God called to him from within the bush, 'Moses! Moses!' And Moses said, 'Here I am.'"

Verse 6: "Then he said, 'I am the God of your father, the God of Abraham, the God of Isaac and the God of Jacob.' At this, Moses hid his face, because he was afraid to look at God."

Note that God identified Moses as a Hebrew son, not as an Egyptian adopted son.

Verse 7: "The Lord said, "I have indeed seen the misery of my people in Egypt. I have heard them crying out because of their slave drivers, and I am concerned about their suffering.

Verse 8: "So I have come down to rescue them from the hand of the Egyptians and to bring them up out of that land into a good and spacious land, a land flowing with milk and honey—the home of the Canaanites, Hittites, Amorites, Perizzites, Hivites and Jebusites.

God made his promise of freedom from oppression and the promise of fertile land through a transfer of land to his people. God had promised this land first to Abraham, the father of Isaac and the grandfather of Jacob, renamed Israel. One of Israel's sons, Joseph, was left to die by his brothers but was saved and raised to power in Egypt. Reconciling, all the brothers moved to Egypt to live in prosperity for a time before becoming enslaved. Through the years of the Israelites' sin toward Joseph, their time of prosperity, and then captivity by Pharaoh, God did not forget them or forget his promise made to their grandfather Abraham. However, it would take over 40 years for them (at least some of them) to arrive and to conquer the Promised Land.

In the history of the Exodus, everyone suffered loss: the Egyptians for their idol worship and refusal to let the Israelites leave their country; the Israelites for their disobedience and idol worship in the wilderness; those who died and lost the land in Israel's quest to conquer the Promised Land; Moses who would not get to enter because of his disobedience; and sadly, God. Through Exodus, God extended his mercy and grace repeatedly, changed his mind about destroying the people for their disloyalty, and rewrote his Commandments for them after being replaced by a gold statue of a calf. Not only did God remember his covenant to Abraham and Moses, he remembered his own desire to establish a relationship with his human creations, faults and all. As much as he tries to guide, command, discipline, and love us, God is continually disappointed by the use of the free will that he gives us. From Adam and Eve through today, the cost of sin is high, so high that God had to intervene and sacrifice his own son, Jesus Christ, to reconcile us back to him. This is a long, sad, faith-filled odyssey that makes me love God even more for his patience and continual efforts to be in a relationship with each one of us.

Verse 9-10: 9 "And now the cry of the Israelites has reached me, and I have seen the way the Egyptians are oppressing them. 10 So now, go. I am sending you to Pharaoh to bring my people the Israelites out of Egypt."

Hearing directly from God comes as an honor but with challenges.

Verse 11: "But Moses said to God, 'Who am I that I should go to Pharaoh and bring the Israelites out of Egypt?'"

Even though God identified Moses as a Hebrew son, Moses continued to question his identity and his role in God's design for Moses and his people.

Verse 12: And God said, "I will be with you. And this will be the sign to you that it is I who have sent you: When you have brought the people out of Egypt, you will worship God on this mountain."

God promised a sign that would come after obedience from Moses, the one who is called, and God commands that Moses will worship God on this mountain.

> *Verse 14: God said to Moses, "I am who I am." This is what you are to say to the Israelites: "I am" has sent me to you.'"*

This is the initial revelation of God's name or identity to Moses.

> *Verse 16: "Go, assemble the elders of Israel and say to them, 'The Lord, the God of your fathers—the God of Abraham, Isaac and Jacob—appeared to me and said: I have watched over you and have seen what has been done to you in Egypt.*

God sent a message to Israel through Moses that he sees them, has watched over them, and knows that they are suffering. This should encourage us to know that even when we are suffering, God is aware and has a plan for us.

From God we hear of promises of "all kinds of miracles". From God came the favor upon the Israelites, who received favor from the Egyptians and gifts to take with them into the desert on their journey. From God came the transfer of wealth from the Egyptians to the Israelites. God's people asked the Egyptians for the best gifts of silver, gold, and fine jewelry, and their requests were granted. God emphasized the importance of worship.

> *Verse 18: "The elders of Israel will listen to you. Then you and the elders are to go to the king of Egypt and say to him, 'The Lord, the God of the Hebrews, has met with us. Let us take a three-day journey into the wilderness to offer sacrifices to the Lord our God.'*

God commanded a 3-day journey into the wilderness to offer sacrifices to him.

Reflection:

1. If God heard the cries of the Hebrew people, and he acted, does this mean that when I cry out to God, he will act on my behalf?

2. Do I know that God sees me and my circumstances?

3. Do I trust God's promises...all of God's promises?

4. Am I free to live a Godly life?

5. How do I address or talk with God? Do I have the familiarity like that of Moses and God?

6. Have I ever had a burning bush experience, holy ground where God spoke to me?

7. Do I worship before I ask for favor AND after God's favor?

Response:

_____

_____

_____

_____

_____

_____

_____

_____

_____

_____

_____

_____

_____

_____

_____

_____

_____

DAY4

Exodus
Chapter Four

Summary:
What if...?

Verse 1: Moses: Moses answered, "What if they do not believe me or listen to me and say, 'The Lord did not appear to you'?"

Verse 2-3: 2 Then the Lord said to him, "What is that in your hand?" "A staff," he replied. 3 The Lord said, "Throw it on the ground." 4 Moses threw it on the ground and it became a snake, and he ran from it.

God asked Moses to use what was available to him. God works miracles through us and through our resources. God's plan was to use Moses to free his people from slavery by transforming a Moses' staff used for shepherding. Moses would go from shepherding sheep to shepherding people. His staff was his symbol of God's authority and his authority. It was used as a weapon and as a sign of miracles by God. Moses' staff was a piece of wood used as a conduit between God and man, much like the cross of Jesus' crucifixion. The wooden staff symbol of the Israelites' freedom from slavery and death parallels the wooden cross symbol of our freedom from sin and death.

Consider the Garden of Eden, the location of the Tree of Life and the Tree of the Knowledge of Good and Evil. Life began in the garden, and Eve and Adam's first sin was eating the fruit from the Tree of Knowledge after being tempted by the serpent. Consider the same elements of nature in the Garden of Eden that come into play as Moses began his role as redeemer of God's people: the wooden staff signified Moses' authority over nature (staff made from the wood of a tree) and the staff that could turn into a serpent and back again by Moses' God-given authority. We can see that God has begun the redemption process to set his people free, in this case, from the Egyptians. It foreshadows the coming of another redeemer who freed God's people from sin and death through Jesus dying on a wooden cross. Verse 5: "This," said the

Lord, "is so that they may believe that the Lord, the God of their fathers—the God of Abraham, the God of Isaac and the God of Jacob—has appeared to you."

Moses was to use signs and wonders to increase the belief of others.

Verse 6: Then the Lord said, "Put your hand inside your cloak." So Moses put his hand into his cloak, and when he took it out, the skin was leprous—it had become as white as snow.

Moses' hand in his cloak became white with disease and then returned to full health. Moses was to use his hands to show that God is a miracle worker, capable of restoring people to full health.

Verse 9: But if they do not believe these two signs or listen to you, take some water from the Nile and pour it on the dry ground. The water you take from the river will become blood on the ground."

The Nile River water turned to blood on the ground. Both water and blood are necessary for humans to live. Egypt relied on the Nile River to survive. The Nile was the lifeblood of Egypt, but God showed that he is the lifeblood of all people.

Verse 10: Moses said to the Lord, "Pardon your servant, Lord. I have never been eloquent, neither in the past nor since you have spoken to your servant. I am slow of speech and tongue."

Moses said that he was tongue-tied, but the Lord decided who was to speak for him. When God calls us to serve him, our excuses are just that: excuses to refuse what he has asked of us. God told Moses that when he calls him, he will also equip him.

Verse 11-12: 11 The Lord said to him, "Who gave human beings their mouths? Who makes them deaf or mute? Who gives them sight or makes them blind? Is it not I, the Lord? 12 Now go; I will help you speak and will teach you what to say."

Verse 13: But Moses said, "Pardon your servant, Lord. Please send someone else."

With the audacity to refuse God, Moses asked God to send anyone else, perhaps a replacement, but God simply sent and equipped Moses' brother Aaron to assist.

Verse 14-17: 14 Then the Lord's anger burned against Moses and he said, "What about your brother, Aaron the Levite? I know he can speak well. He is already on his way to meet you, and he will be glad to see you. 15 You shall speak to him and put words in his mouth; I will help both of you speak and will teach you what to do. 16 He will speak to the people for you, and it will be as if he were your mouth and as if you were God to him. 17 But take this staff in your hand so you can perform the signs with it."

Angry at Moses' reticence to accept his calling, God ADDS Aaron to ASSIST, not to REPLACE. (I think Moses may have been surprised at this strategy. Well played, Lord!) Aaron becomes the mouth, the interpreter for Moses.

God gave Moses both the brother and the staff as aids for Moses' mission to return to Egypt.

Verse 19-20: 19 Now the Lord had said to Moses in Midian, "Go back to Egypt, for all those who wanted to kill you are dead." 20 So Moses took his wife and sons, put them on a donkey and started back to Egypt. And he took the staff of God in his hand.

Notice that this is the first time that Moses' staff is called the "staff of God". This staff was going to be used to show God's authority and power many times in the life of Moses and the Israelites.

We see a parallel of this image of Moses with his wife and children on a donkey going toward Egypt to save Israel, described by God as God's firstborn son (as the favored nation). In the New

Testament, we see Joseph with his wife Mary and baby Jesus traveling toward Egypt to save Jesus, God's only begotten son, from being murdered by Herod.

Verse 21-23: 21 The Lord said to Moses, "When you return to Egypt, see that you perform before Pharaoh all the wonders I have given you the power to do. But I will harden his heart so that he will not let the people go. 22 Then say to Pharaoh, 'This is what the Lord says: Israel is my firstborn son, 23 and I told you, "Let my son go, so he may worship me." But you refused to let him go; so I will kill your firstborn son.'"

Verse 24: At a lodging place on the way, the Lord met Moses and was about to kill him.

Not only was God angry with Moses for refusing his assignment, Moses had not circumcised his son, according to the law. Moses' wife, Zipporah, rescued Moses and her son by performing circumcision on him. This action redeemed her husband, son, and their bloodline.

In today's culture, this same sin of neglecting the spiritual education of children is often committed by parents. It's not too late to start now to save them and their bloodline!

Verse 25-26: 25 But Zipporah took a flint knife, cut off her son's foreskin and touched Moses' feet with it. "Surely you are a bridegroom of blood to me," she said. 26 So the Lord let him alone. (At that time she said "bridegroom of blood," referring to circumcision.)

The purpose of the exodus out of Egypt is to free the people from bondage in order to worship God. On the way to Egypt, the Lord confronted Moses and was about to kill him. Zipporah circumcised her son, and then the Lord left him alone. It was a blood sacrifice to God for the atonement of Moses' protests and disobedience. Moses hadn't followed the law of circumcision for his generation. A lesson here for leaders is that when they are called by God, they are to lead or God will get them out of the way.

> *Verse 27: The Lord said to Aaron, "Go into the wilderness to meet Moses." So he met Moses at the mountain of God and kissed him.*

No protests or excuses from Aaron. God said go, so Aaron went...

> *Verse 29-31: 29 Moses and Aaron brought together all the elders of the Israelites, 30 and Aaron told them everything the Lord had said to Moses. He also performed the signs before the people, 31 and they believed. And when they heard that the Lord was concerned about them and had seen their misery, they bowed down and worshiped.*

God sees us and our circumstances, both our joy and our misery.

Reflection:

1. Moses and Aaron told all the elders of Israel what the Lord had told them, and they performed miraculous signs to support God's message. What is the Lord telling me to tell others? What miraculous signs is God wanting to do through me?

2. When has God called me to do something for him, and I have protested?

3. What do I have on hand or in hand to demonstrate God's power and love?

4. When have I been sure that God sees me?

5. Who is my Moses or my Aaron, who helps me to obey God or to lead others from bondage to freedom to worship God?

6. God makes the impossible possible. "What is that in your hand?" What do we have available to us that we can use for

God or to show God's power?

7. When have I been asked by God to take what's in my hand and throw it to the ground in front of unbelievers?

Response:

_____

_____

_____

_____

_____

_____

_____

_____

_____

DAY**5**

Exodus
Chapter Five

Summary:
Let us go or...

Verse 1: Afterward Moses and Aaron went to Pharaoh and said, "This is what the Lord, the God of Israel, says: 'Let my people go, so that they may hold a festival to me in the wilderness.'"

Moses' request was to free God's people for a specific purpose, "so that" they may honor God.

Verse 3: Then they said, "The God of the Hebrews has met with us. Now let us take a three-day journey into the wilderness to offer sacrifices to the Lord our God, or he may strike us with plagues or with the sword."

Verse 4: But the king of Egypt said, "Moses and Aaron, why are you taking the people away from their labor? Get back to your work!"

Pharaoh turned blame onto Moses and Aaron: "Why are you distracting the people from their tasks?"

Verse 7: "You are no longer to supply the people with straw for making bricks; let them go and gather their own straw.

Repercussion/consequence for Moses' request: no more straw for bricks - make the people get it themselves - but same number as before. Pharaoh turns blame onto the people, saying that they are lazy.

Condescension - "They are lazy."

Increased Oppression - "Load them down!"

Physically Pressed - "Make them sweat."

Verse 12: So the people scattered all over Egypt to gather stubble to use for straw.

Verse 14: And Pharaoh's slave drivers beat the Israelite overseers they had appointed, demanding, "Why haven't you met your quota of bricks yesterday or today, as before?"

Pharaoh punished the leaders of the people. Israelite foremen were whipped. They pleaded to Pharaoh. Pharaoh's response: You're just lazy! Lazy!

Verse 20: When they left Pharaoh, they found Moses and Aaron waiting to meet them, 21 and they said, "May the Lord look on you and judge you! You have made us obnoxious to Pharaoh and his officials and have put a sword in their hand to kill us."

Israelite foremen confronted and cursed Moses and Aaron: "May the Lord punish YOU!"

Verse 22: Moses returned to the Lord and said, "Why, Lord, why have you brought trouble on this people? Is this why you sent me? 23 Ever since I went to Pharaoh to speak in your name, he has brought trouble on this people, and you have not rescued your people at all."

Moses then confronted the Lord: Why? Why? Why did you send me? (Protest.) "And you have done nothing to rescue them" NIV or "And you have done nothing at all!" NLT

Sometimes life gets harder before getting better. God's ways are not always clear nor easy. In the New Testament, Jesus warned the disciples of difficult times to come, but we often choose not to hear the difficult parts of God's plan for us as Jesus followers. We typically ask "why" when asked to do something hard.

Matthew 24:9 "Then you will be handed over to be persecuted and put to death, and you will be hated by all nations because of me.

Reflection:

1. Was God preparing the way for the Israelites to WANT to leave Egypt by making life more difficult for them? Does God prompt changes in our lives through temporary hardships?

- (See 12:33 The Egyptians urged the people to hurry and leave the country. "For otherwise," they said, "we will all die!"

- 12:40 The Israelites had lived there for 430 years!

- 13:18 God led them through the wilderness.

- 14:2 Then they had to turn back and camp...

- 14:11 Didn't we tell you this would happen while we were still in Egypt? We said, "Leave us alone! Let us be slaves to the Egyptians. It's better to be a slave in Egypt than a corpse in the wilderness!")

2. Have I had times of wanting to stay behind when God wanted me to move forward in my life? Did I want to stay in poor circumstances because I was familiar with my condition? Was I stuck for so many years that I couldn't see God providing a way out? Do I prefer a poor known situation to a better unknown that God has for me?

3. God frees us from oppression SO THAT we may honor him. When have I been freed from oppression, and how have I honored God for my freedom?

4. When have I obeyed God but was misunderstood or punished for trying?

5. What distracts me from doing my tasks?

6. Define "laziness" (they do not want to work - give effort.)

7. When in my life have I asked God, "Why? Why? Why did you send me?"

Response:

_____

_____

_____

_____

_____

_____

_____

_____

_____

_____

_____

_____

DAY**6**

Exodus
Chapter Six

Summary:
God's promises of deliverance.

Verse 1: Then the Lord said to Moses, "Now you will see what I will do to Pharaoh: Because of my mighty hand he will let them go; because of my mighty hand he will drive them out of his country."

God took the credit for Pharaoh letting the people go and for forcing them to leave the land.

Verse 2-5: God also said to Moses, "I am the Lord 3 I appeared to Abraham, to Isaac and to Jacob as God Almighty, but by my name the Lord. I did not make myself fully known to them. 4 I also established my covenant with them to give them the land of Canaan, where they resided as foreigners. 5 Moreover, I have heard the groaning of the Israelites, whom the Egyptians are enslaving, and I have remembered my covenant.

God reassured Moses of who he is, of his covenant with Moses' ancestors, of his promise to give the Promised Land, that he has heard their groanings, and that he has remembered his covenant.

Verse 6-8: "Therefore, say to the Israelites: 'I am the Lord, and I will bring you out from under the yoke of the Egyptians. I will free you from being slaves to them, and I will redeem you with an outstretched arm and with mighty acts of judgment. 7 I will take you as my own people, and I will be your God. Then you will know that I am the Lord your God, who brought you out from under the yoke of the Egyptians. 8 And I will bring you to the land I swore with an uplifted hand to give to Abraham, to Isaac and to Jacob. I will give it to you as a possession. I am the Lord.'"

God's promises of deliverance.

I will FREE you.

I will RESCUE you.

I will REDEEM you.

I will CLAIM you.

I will BE YOUR GOD.

I will BRING YOU INTO THE LAND

I will GIVE IT TO YOU

I AM THE LORD.

Verse 9: Moses reported this to the Israelites, but they did not listen to him because of their discouragement and harsh labor.

Moses delivered God's message, but the people refused to listen. Sometimes people had difficulty hearing the salvation message because of physical or emotional distress.

Verse 12: But Moses said to the Lord, "If the Israelites will not listen to me, why would Pharaoh listen to me, since I speak with faltering lips?"

Moses struggled with his disability or weakness because even his own people did not listen to him. How would he expect the great Pharaoh to listen to him? Moses was whining, protesting, or doubting his own abilities, once again to the Lord.

Verse 13: Now the Lord spoke to Moses and Aaron about the Israelites and Pharaoh king of Egypt, and he commanded them to bring the Israelites out of Egypt.

What follows is the list of ancestors of Moses and Aaron, confirming once again that they were worthy and notable to lead the people out of Egypt. These are the people (God's people). Since I connected with the tribe of Levi, I noted that Levi lived to be 137 years old.

Verse 30: But Moses said to the Lord, "Since I speak with faltering lips, why would Pharaoh listen to me?"

Moses continued to protest to the Lord: "I can't do it! Why should Pharaoh listen?" Moses dwelt on his disability rather than on his trust that the Lord and Aaron would be there with him.

Reflection:

1. What are God's promises that I have experienced?
2. Which is the most difficult to accept?
   - Freedom?
   - Rescue from present circumstances?
   - Redemption?
   - Bringing you into new land?
   - Giving you new land?
   - Being your God?
3. Why?
4. When have I told God, "I can do it!"?
5. When have I degraded myself before God, citing my weaknesses as excuses to serve him in a particular way when he called me?
6. When have I not accepted responsibility for God's commands to lead or to represent him?

We are all called to represent God with our words, actions, staffs, abilities, etc. We can learn from Moses that God does not accept excuses when we are called into service. However, God does help us when we sincerely ask for help in our weakness.

Response:

_____

_____

_____

_____

_____

_____

_____

_____

_____

_____

_____

_____

_____

DAY**7**

Exodus
Chapter Seven

Summary:

The signs and wonders begin before Pharaoh.

Verse 1: Then the Lord said to Moses, "See, I have made you like God to Pharaoh, and your brother Aaron will be your prophet.

Through the signs and wonders from God through Moses, God was the great equalizer of power between Moses and Pharaoh, telling Moses that he is like God to Pharaoh. Aaron was elevated to the status of prophet by God. God told Moses, and Aaron told Pharaoh. As with Moses and Aaron, when God chooses to use us for his purposes, he empowers us and gives us a feeling of equal footing to our adversaries.

Verse 3-5: But I will harden Pharaoh's heart, and though I multiply my signs and wonders in Egypt, he will not listen to you. Then I will lay my hand on Egypt and with mighty acts of judgment I will bring out my divisions, my people the Israelites. 5 And the Egyptians will know that I am the Lord when I stretch out my hand against Egypt and bring the Israelites out of it."

God made Pharaoh's heart hard "so I can multiply my miraculous signs and wonders in the land of Egypt." God multiplies! God rescues, and God judges.

Verse 7: Moses was eighty years old and Aaron eighty-three when they spoke to Pharaoh.

Let that sink in for a minute. At 80 and 83 years of age, Moses and Aaron had the strength, wisdom, and purpose to fulfill their calling and to face down Pharaoh.

Verse 8-9: The Lord said to Moses and Aaron, 9 "When Pharaoh says to you, 'Perform a miracle,' then say to Aaron, 'Take your staff and throw it down before Pharaoh,' and it will become a snake."

God said that Pharaoh will demand a miracle and prepared Moses and Aaron. "Say to Aaron, take your staff and throw it down" in front of Pharaoh (see 4:2)

Verse 11: Pharaoh then summoned wise men and sorcerers, and the Egyptian magicians also did the same things by their secret arts:

Pharaoh's wise men and sorcerers/magicians did the same. The occult can mimic spiritual power, unless God intervenes.

Verse 12: Each one threw down his staff and it became a snake. But Aaron's staff swallowed up their staffs.

Aaron's staff swallowed up their serpents (4:3 was Moses' staff to a serpent) Sometimes God surprises even us! Apparently Moses and Aaron were surprised as well.

Verse 15: Go to Pharaoh in the morning as he goes out to the river. Confront him on the bank of the Nile, and take in your hand the staff that was changed into a snake.

God told Moses to take along the staff that turned into a snake (Aaron's staff). This staff was going to continue to hold significant power when used as a sign of authority from God.

God demonstrated his power and his will through this staff. In Numbers 17 when God told Moses to take a staff from each of the tribes of Israel and place them in the tent of the covenant law to discern whom God would choose as leader, God told Moses to write Aaron's name on the staff of Levi, the tribal name of Moses and Aaron.

Numbers 17: 1-11: 1 The Lord said to Moses, 2 "Speak to the Israelites and get twelve staffs from them, one from the leader of each of their ancestral tribes. Write the name of each man on his staff. 3 On the staff of Levi write Aaron's name, for there must be one staff for the head of each ancestral tribe. 4 Place them in the tent of meeting in front of the ark of the covenant law, where I meet with you. 5 The staff belonging to the man I choose will sprout, and I will rid myself of this constant grumbling against you by the Israelites." 6 So Moses spoke to the Israelites, and their leaders gave him twelve staffs, one for the leader of each of their ancestral tribes, and Aaron's staff was among them. 7 Moses placed the staffs before the Lord in the tent of the covenant law. 8 The next day Moses entered the tent and saw that Aaron's staff, which represented the tribe of Levi, had not only sprouted but had budded, blossomed and produced almonds. 9 Then Moses brought out all the staffs from the Lord's presence to all the Israelites. They looked at them, and each of the leaders took his own staff. 10 The Lord said to Moses, "Put back Aaron's staff in front of the ark of the covenant law, to be kept as a sign to the rebellious. This will put an end to their grumbling against me, so that they will not die." 11 Moses did just as the Lord commanded him. Verse 15-18: Go to Pharaoh in the morning as he goes out to the river. Confront him on the bank of the Nile, and take in your hand the staff that was changed into a snake. 16 Then say to him, 'The Lord, the God of the Hebrews, has sent me to say to you: Let my people go, so that they may worship me in the wilderness. But until now you have not listened. 17 This is what the Lord says: By this you will know that I am the Lord: With the staff that is in my hand I will strike the water of the Nile, and it will be changed into blood. 18 The fish in the Nile will die, and the river will stink; the Egyptians will not be able to drink its water.'"

The mission for Moses from the Lord was to go, confront Pharaoh, take his staff, and speak God's words to Pharaoh. Note that the Lord's words, as quoted by Moses, say, "with the staff that is in MY hand, I will strike the water of the Nile, and it will be changed into blood." God emphasizes that the staff is in God's hands and that God will strike the water. God is to get the glory for what is about to happen. We are also called to go into the world, to confront sin in the world, to take our staff (the Bible), and to speak God's words.

Verse 19: The Lord said to Moses, "Tell Aaron, 'Take your staff and stretch out your hand over the waters of Egypt—over the streams and canals, over the ponds and all the reservoirs—and they will turn to blood.' Blood will be everywhere in Egypt, even in vessels of wood and stone."

It is significant that the power of God stretched beyond the banks of the bodies of water and into the vessels of wood and stone that would be located in people's homes and in the palace. God's power and influence was to be felt everywhere with everyone.

It is also significant that the Lord commanded Moses to tell Aaron to use his staff to turn the water to blood. Originally, Aaron was appointed as Moses' assistant because Moses said that he had trouble speaking. This action involved no words, no speaking, yet Aaron was appointed to make it happen. I wonder what Moses thought about his brother taking the lead in this miracle. There is no record of Moses protesting God's choice here. We did read that when Aaron was asked to go with Moses, he went. He did not protest or question God. Perhaps it was important for God to draft the man that acted without question in this circumstance.

Verse 20: Moses and Aaron did just as the Lord had commanded. He raised his staff in the presence of Pharaoh and his officials and struck the water of the Nile, and all the water was changed into blood.

Aaron raised his staff and struck the water of the Nile:

Fish died (man's actions affect the climate and health of all).

Water turned foul - undrinkable.

Blood was everywhere.

Egyptians had to dig along the riverbank for drinkable water.

Verse 22: But the Egyptian magicians did the same things by their secret arts, and Pharaoh's heart became hard; he would not listen to Moses and Aaron, just as the Lord had said.

Magicians copied the miracle.

Reflection:

1. Will I still be walking with God and leading at age 80?

2. Have I ever seen a miracle in nature that helped me to believe in God?

3. In what ways do human's actions affect our environment and health?

4. Pharaoh said, "Show me a miracle!" Has that ever happened today, where someone asks for proof through a miracle? How did God respond? How did the person respond?

The first proof by God is given to Moses in Chapter 4.

The second proof by God is given to Pharaoh in Chapter 7.

Response:

_____

_____

_____

_____

_____

_____

_____

_____

_____

_____

_____

_____

_____

DAY**8**

Exodus
Chapter Eight

Summary:

Verse 1-4: 1 Then the Lord said to Moses, "Go to Pharaoh and say to him, 'This is what the Lord says: Let my people go, so that they may worship me. 2 If you refuse to let them go, I will send a plague of frogs on your whole country. 3 The Nile will teem with frogs. They will come up into your palace and your bedroom and onto your bed, into the houses of your officials and on your people, and into your ovens and kneading troughs. 4 The frogs will come up on you and your people and all your officials.'"

Just like the plague of the Nile turning to blood and beyond, with even water in vessels turning to blood, God extended the plague of frogs beyond the Nile and into the palace, homes, beds, ovens, and kneading troughs of the people. They invaded places where people sleep and eat. The two plagues personally affected the people to the core and into their personal spaces. No one was exempt. The whole kingdom from Pharaoh to his officials to all the people were affected by the practices of the land and the decisions of the king. Isn't this just like our present political circumstances? The practices of our country and the decisions of our national leaders affects all of us, from the president to the officials to the people. We are all affected by poor decisions and lifestyles that go against God's commands.

Verse 5: Then the Lord said to Moses, "Tell Aaron, 'Stretch out your hand with your staff over the streams and canals and ponds, and make frogs come up on the land of Egypt.'"

Again, it is Aaron who was appointed to work the miracle plague of the frogs. Once he was told, he obeyed without question or protest.

Verse 6: So Aaron stretched out his hand over the waters of Egypt, and the frogs came up and covered the land.

Verse 7: But the magicians did the same things by their secret arts; they also made frogs come up on the land of Egypt.

Again Pharaoh's magicians were able to copy the plague of the frogs. Because of their desire to disprove God, apparently the land ended up with twice as many frogs. I doubt that the people appreciated a double dose of frog legs!

Verse 8: Pharaoh summoned Moses and Aaron and said, "Pray to the Lord to take the frogs away from me and my people, and I will let your people go to offer sacrifices to the Lord."

Pharaoh summoned and begged Moses and Aaron to pray to God for him, thus acknowledging the existence and the power of God. This is the first recorded time that Pharaoh acknowledges the Lord.

Verse 9: Moses said to Pharaoh, "I leave to you the honor of setting the time for me to pray for you and your officials and your people that you and your houses may be rid of the frogs, except for those that remain in the Nile."

Moses gave Pharaoh the honor of setting the time to end the plague of frogs. Interestingly, Pharaoh chose "Tomorrow." What was the point of postponing the plague? I wonder why Pharaoh didn't say, "Immediately!" (See 9:5 For the next plague, the Lord will set the time!)

Verse 12-13: 12 After Moses and Aaron left Pharaoh, Moses cried out to the Lord about the frogs he had brought on Pharaoh. 13 And the Lord did what Moses asked. The frogs died in the houses, in the courtyards and in the fields.

Verse 14: They were piled into heaps, and the land reeked of them.

Just because the plague came to an end didn't mean that the suffering stopped. There was the removal of all the frogs and the stench from all the dead frogs. When God hears our cries for help to stop pain and suffering, there may still be residual effects or consequences. Sometimes there is work left for the people to do, even after God answers our prayers.

Verse 15: But when Pharaoh saw that there was relief, he hardened his heart and would not listen to Moses and Aaron, just as the Lord had said.

Pharaoh saw relief and recanted on his promise. Sometimes we do the same. When we cry out to God to heal a situation, and God responds, we get comfortable and forget God's mercy, perhaps recanting or breaking promises made during our prayer requests. How soon we forget when the crisis is over. We, like Pharaoh, quickly go back to our old habits or beliefs.

Verse 16-18: 16 Then the Lord said to Moses, "Tell Aaron, 'Stretch out your staff and strike the dust of the ground,' and throughout the land of Egypt the dust will become gnats." 17 They did this, and when Aaron stretched out his hand with the staff and struck the dust of the ground, gnats came on people and animals. All the dust throughout the land of Egypt became gnats. 18 But when the magicians tried to produce gnats by their secret arts, they could not.

Annoying gnats as numerous as grains of dust came on both people and animals. The poor animals had to suffer along with the humans. This time, though, Pharaoh's magicians could not replicate the plague!

Verse 19: the magicians said to Pharaoh, "This is the finger of God." But Pharaoh's heart was hard and he would not listen, just as the Lord had said.

Because the magicians could not replicate this plague, they acknowledged the existence and power of God. They believed! Pharaoh must have been both disappointed and embarrassed by the magicians' failure and testimony, yet he refused to listen. The same thing happens when non-Christians witness God's signs and wonders, yet they refuse to acknowledge God.

In Jesus' story of the rich man in Hades and Lazarus in heaven with Abraham, the rich man begs Lazarus to warn his family about the consequences of sin. Abraham acknowledges that some people refuse to listen and to repent, even if someone rises from the dead.

Luke 16:27-31: 27 "He answered, 'Then I beg you, father, send Lazarus to my family, 28 for I have five brothers. Let him warn them, so that they will not also come to this place of torment.' 29 "Abraham replied, 'They have Moses and the Prophets; let them listen to them.' 30 "'No, father Abraham,' he said, 'but if someone from the dead goes to them, they will repent.' 31 "He said to him, 'If they do not listen to Moses and the Prophets, they will not be convinced even if someone rises from the dead.'"

Verse 20: Then the Lord said to Moses, "Get up early in the morning and confront Pharaoh as he goes to the river and say to him, 'This is what the Lord says: Let my people go, so that they may worship me.

God commanded Moses and Aaron to rise early and to get in Pharaoh's face while he was making his way to the river. This must have been a bold and dangerous move that could have cost them their lives, but God protected them.

Verse 22-23: 22 "'But on that day I will deal differently with the land of Goshen, where my people live; no swarms of flies will be there, so that you will know that I, the Lord, am in this land. 23 I will make a distinction between my people and your people. This sign will occur tomorrow.'"

This was the first plague where God made a distinction between the Israelites and the Egyptians. This time the Israelites did not have to suffer. This time God dictated the time for the plague to start. God was present in ALL the land, but differentiated the locality of Goshen and spared them. God was showing territorial power. Even with us today, if we follow God's commands, we receive blessings from what separates us from the rest of the world. May we use these blessings as ways to bless others and to give glory to God.

Verse 24: And the Lord did this. Dense swarms of flies poured into Pharaoh's palace and into the houses of his officials; throughout Egypt the land was ruined by the flies.

Imagine the numbers of flies that had to be present to completely destroy the land of Egypt!

Verse 25: Then Pharaoh summoned Moses and Aaron and said, "Go, sacrifice to your God here in the land."

Pharaoh wanted to negotiate with Moses and Aaron by allowing sacrifices to God but wanting them to agree to a partial concession based on territorial or geographical lines.

Verse 26-27: 26 But Moses said, "That would not be right. The sacrifices we offer the Lord our God would be detestable to the Egyptians. And if we offer sacrifices that are detestable in their eyes, will they not stone us? 27 We must take a three-day journey into the wilderness to offer sacrifices to the Lord our God, as he commands us."

Moses knew his Egyptian roots and practices enough to know that offering sacrifices on Pharaoh's land would result in stoning (persecution)? He knew wisely that they must take the 3-day trip to the wilderness as God commanded.

Verse 28: Pharaoh said, "I will let you go to offer sacrifices to the Lord your God in the wilderness, but you must not go very far. Now pray for me."

Next Pharaoh conceded to allow the people to go but not too far. He also asked for prayer, again seeming to acknowledge the God of Moses and Aaron. This sounds like what we call a "foxhole prayer" where folks only pray when they are in immediate danger or discomfort.

Verse 29: Moses answered, "As soon as I leave you, I will pray to the Lord, and tomorrow the flies will leave Pharaoh and his officials and his people. Only let Pharaoh be sure that he does not act deceitfully again by not letting the people go to offer sacrifices to the Lord."

This sounds like a warning from Moses to Pharaoh not to deceive the people again.

Hardness of Heart: God vs. Pharaoh

1. Snakes: a sign that had no effect on Pharaoh
2. Blood Water: Sign that affected the people (They had to dig for clear water.)
3. Frogs: Sign that brought acknowledgment of God.
4. Gnats: Sign that caused others (magicians) to believe
5. Flies: Sign that put God right in Pharaoh's way
6. Sign that shows God's people are saved/blessed (no flies in Goshen)
7. Pharaoh wants to negotiate with God on his terms. No! Pharaoh asks for prayer just to be relieved of temporary discomfort.

Reflection:

1. When have I cried out to the Lord for relief?

2. When have I wanted to worship the Lord on my own terms?

3. When have I said a "foxhole prayer" in time of need? When have I tried to negotiate with God with promises if he answers my cry?

4. When have I made God a promise and then recanted? When have I repented, found relief, and recanted or turned back to my former evil ways?

5. When have I asked others to pray for me, but I have not prayed for them myself?

6. When has God asked me to go - to meet someone - you say why I was sent - and to speak a word of God over them or to them?

Response:

_____

_____

_____

_____

_____

_____

_____

DAY**9**

Exodus
Chapter Nine

Summary:

This time Moses gave no warning and no words directly to Pharaoh.

Verse 1: Then the Lord said to Moses, "Go to Pharaoh and say to him, 'This is what the Lord, the God of the Hebrews, says: "Let my people go, so that they may worship me."

God identified as "the God of the Hebrews" Warning - plague on livestock.

Verse 4: But the Lord will make a distinction between the livestock of Israel and that of Egypt, so that no animal belonging to the Israelites will die.'"

Distinction again between Israelites and Egyptians

Verse 5: The Lord set a time and said, "Tomorrow the Lord will do this in the land.

This time the Lord set the time - tomorrow (in 8:9 Moses let Pharaoh set the time)

Verse 6: And the next day the Lord did it: All the livestock of the Egyptians died, but not one animal belonging to the Israelites died.

The Lord did just as he said. God is a God of promises!

Verse 7: Pharaoh investigated and found that not even one of the animals of the Israelites had died. Yet his heart was unyielding and he would not let the people go.

Pharaoh sent officials to investigate. Now the officials have a testimony as well!

Verse 8: Then the Lord said to Moses and Aaron, "Take handfuls of soot from a furnace and have Moses toss it into the air in the presence of Pharaoh.

This time, instead of Aaron raising the staff, both Aaron and Moses took action to make the plague happen. By taking soot from a brick kiln, Moses and Aaron were using material associated with the slavery of the Israelites to punish the slave masters, the Egyptians. The soot affected both people and animals. (Again, the animals had to suffer for people's sin).

Verse 10: So they took soot from a furnace and stood before Pharaoh. Moses tossed it into the air, and festering boils broke out on people and animals.

The source of suffering of the Israelites was to become the source of suffering for the Egyptians. The dust fell on their skin and got into their lungs - a plague on the outside and inside of the body. The soot was thrown from the sky: symbolic of coming from God and not humans (Moses or Aaron). The miracle of multiplication: the few handfuls of soot covered the whole land of Egypt.

Verse 11: The magicians could not stand before Moses because of the boils that were on them and on all the Egyptians.

Not only could the magicians not copy this plague, but they themselves were unable to stand.

Verse 13-14: 13 Then the Lord said to Moses, "Get up early in the morning, confront Pharaoh and say to him, 'This is what the Lord, the God of the Hebrews, says: Let my people go, so that they may worship me, 14 or this time I will send the full force of my plagues against you and against your officials and your people, so you may know that there is no one like me in all the earth.

The warnings heightened to hailstorms!

Verse 16: But I have raised you up for this very purpose, that I might show you my power and that my name might be proclaimed in all the earth.

Sometimes God raises up leaders to show his power and to have his name proclaimed. For Pharaoh, he was raised up to be destroyed because he refused to listen to the word of God.

Verse 17-19: 17 You still set yourself against my people and will not let them go. 18 Therefore, at this time tomorrow I will send the worst hailstorm that has ever fallen on Egypt, from the day it was founded till now. 19 Give an order now to bring your livestock and everything you have in the field to a place of shelter, because the hail will fall on every person and animal that has not been brought in and is still out in the field, and they will die.'"

Verse 20-21: 20 Those officials of Pharaoh who feared the word of the Lord hurried to bring their slaves and their livestock inside. 21 But those who ignored the word of the Lord left their slaves and livestock in the field.

There was evidence of Pharaoh's officials being divided in their beliefs. Some officials were afraid and complied. Others paid no attention.

Verse 22: Then the Lord said to Moses, "Stretch out your hand toward the sky so that hail will fall all over Egypt—on people and animals and on everything growing in the fields of Egypt."

Verse 23: When Moses stretched out his staff toward the sky, the Lord sent thunder and hail, and lightning flashed down to the ground. So the Lord rained hail on the land of Egypt;

This time it is Moses alone, without mention of Aaron, who lifted his hand/staff for the hailstorm that left Egypt in ruins. (Are we witnesses to even the faith of Moses increasing through these signs?) People, animals, plants were destroyed, except in Goshen, the land of the Israelites.

Verse 26: The only place it did not hail was the land of Goshen, where the Israelites were.

God made a distinction between the Egyptians and the Israelites.

Verse 27: Then Pharaoh summoned Moses and Aaron. "This time I have sinned," he said to them. "The Lord is in the right, and I and my people are in the wrong.

Pharaoh repented for himself and extended this to his people.

Verse 28: Pray to the Lord, for we have had enough thunder and hail. I will let you go; you don't have to stay any longer."

Pharaoh said that he conceded, but he did not.

Verse 29-30: 29 Moses replied, "When I have gone out of the city, I will spread out my hands in prayer to the Lord. The thunder will stop and there will be no more hail, so you may know that the earth is the Lord's. But I know that you and your officials still do not fear the Lord God."

Verse 34: When Pharaoh saw that the rain and hail and thunder had stopped, he sinned again: He and his officials hardened their hearts.

Verse 35: So Pharaoh's heart was hard and he would not let the Israelites go, just as the Lord had said through Moses.

Reflection:

1. What must Pharaoh have thought about Moses' one God as compared to Pharaoh's 50+ gods? Did he think that sheer numbers of idols were more powerful than God?

2. What is the significance of soot from a brick kiln? (bricks=slavery)

3. When the officials were warned to come in from the fields, why did some choose to obey while others chose to ignore the warning?

4. What distinctions can be seen today between God's chosen people and the rest of the world? Are there any distinctions that everyone can see or know?

5. What step was missing in Pharaoh's frequent expressions of repentance?

Response:

_____

_____

_____

_____

_____

_____

_____

_____

DAY**10**

Exodus
Chapter Ten

Summary:

Verse 1-2: 1 Then the Lord said to Moses, "Go to Pharaoh, for I have hardened his heart and the hearts of his officials so that I may perform these signs of mine among them 2 that you may tell your children and grandchildren how I dealt harshly with the Egyptians and how I performed my signs among them, and that you may know that I am the Lord."

While the Pyramids serve as part of Egyptian history, the Exodus is part of our Christian oral history. Note the dual emphasis on what is significant to the different cultures. The ancient kings desired physical monuments to memorialize them, but the God of the Israelites desired the spiritual monument as a testament to the person and power of God. The Pyramids are tributes to Egyptian kings with their dead bodies and wealthy possessions. The oral and written history of God passed down through generations is a tribute to the Living God, his power and desire for relationships with his people.

Consider, also, the teaching of Jesus in the New Testament regarding the difference between the kingdom of the world and the kingdom of God.

John 18:36 Jesus said, "My kingdom is not of this world. If it were, my servants would fight to prevent my arrest by the Jewish leaders. But now my kingdom is from another place."

Verse 3: So Moses and Aaron went to Pharaoh and said to him, "This is what the Lord, the God of the Hebrews, says: 'How long will you refuse to humble yourself before me? Let my people go, so that they may worship me.

In verse 6, Moses predicted that the locusts would devour all the trees in the fields in a plague worse than any that Pharaoh's ancestors had seen. Then Moses and Aaron left the palace.

Verse 7: Pharaoh's officials said to him, "How long will this man be a snare to us? Let the people go, so that they may worship the Lord their God. Do you not yet realize that Egypt is ruined?"

What an ironic statement since they are holding the Israelites hostage (reversed slavery language) The officials realized that Egypt was losing the struggle with God while Pharaoh must be in denial. "Don't you realize that Egypt lies in ruin?" So much so that Pharaoh brought Moses and Aaron back to ask for details of their request to leave.

Verse 8: Then Moses and Aaron were brought back to Pharaoh. "Go, worship the Lord your God," he said. "But tell me who will be going."

Verse 10-11: 10 Pharaoh said, "The Lord be with you—if I let you go, along with your women and children! Clearly you are bent on evil. 11 No! Have only the men go and worship the Lord, since that's what you have been asking for." Then Moses and Aaron were driven out of Pharaoh's presence.

Pharaoh showed limited compliance and misconstrued Moses' request to let men, women, and children go. Then he threw Moses and Aaron out.

Verse 13: So Moses stretched out his staff over Egypt, and the Lord made an east wind blow across the land all that day and all that night. By morning the wind had brought the locusts;

Moses raised his staff over Egypt. Locusts devoured every plant.

Verse 16-17: 16 Pharaoh quickly summoned Moses and Aaron and said, "I have sinned against the Lord your God and against you. 17 Now forgive my sin once more and pray to the Lord your God to take this deadly plague away from me."

Moses and Aaron were thrown out before the plague of locusts; then they were QUICKLY summoned back by Pharaoh for another fast repentance request to get the locusts to stop.

Verse 21: Then the Lord said to Moses, "Stretch out your hand toward the sky so that darkness spreads over Egypt—darkness that can be felt."

Darkness for three days, but Goshen had light.

Verse 23: No one could see anyone else or move about for three days. Yet all the Israelites had light in the places where they lived.

Verse 24: Then Pharaoh summoned Moses and said, "Go, worship the Lord. Even your women and children may go with you; only leave your flocks and herds behind."

Pharaoh conceded the children but wanted to hang on to the flocks, the livestock.

Verse 25: But Moses said, "You must allow us to have sacrifices and burnt offerings to present to the Lord our God.

At this point, Moses was demanding supplies as well as freedom.

Verse 26: Our livestock too must go with us; not a hoof is to be left behind. We have to use some of them in worshiping the Lord our God, and until we get there we will not know what we are to use to worship the Lord."

Verse 28: Pharaoh said to Moses, "Get out of my sight! Make sure you do not appear before me again! The day you see my face you will die."

Go and don't come back? Note 11:4 where Moses came back and didn't die!

Reflection:

1. How important is it to tell our children and grandchildren about our family history and what God has done for us? Which narrative do I live by: the Kingdom of the World of physical monuments of wealth and power or the Kingdom of God with spiritual monuments of God's power and salvation of souls?

2. Do you know someone who is suffering greatly because they refuse to submit to God, yet they continue to think that they are in control of their lives? What needs to change for them to understand how God works and who God is?

3. When the world seems to be in complete darkness, do I know that I can live in the light of God? How can I be a light in a dark world?

4. How does God distinguish his people from the rest of the world much like the Israelites were allowed to live in the light while all the rest of Egypt was in total darkness?

5. When have I complied with part of what God wants me to do, but then I want to hold back some of myself for myself?

6. When have I followed God without knowing exactly what will happen in the future? When have I gone forward before knowing all the details?

7. Sometimes God supplies us with things from the world that we can use for his purpose and glory. For example, companies with excess products donate to churches to distribute to the needy so that the companies can write it off their taxes. Has anything similar ever happened in my experience?

Response:

_____

_____

_____

_____

_____

_____

_____

_____

_____

_____

_____

_____

_____

DAY**11**

Exodus
Chapter Eleven

Summary:

Verse 1: Now the Lord had said to Moses, "I will bring one more plague on Pharaoh and on Egypt. After that, he will let you go from here, and when he does, he will drive you out completely.

Pharaoh changed his tactics. He forced all to leave rather than just "permitting" them to leave.

Verse 3: (The Lord made the Egyptians favorably disposed toward the people, and Moses himself was highly regarded in Egypt by Pharaoh's officials and by the people.)

Moses had found favor from Pharaoh's officials and the Egyptian people.

Verse 5: Every firstborn son in Egypt will die, from the firstborn son of Pharaoh, who sits on the throne, to the firstborn son of the female slave, who is at her hand mill, and all the firstborn of the cattle as well.

God showed how comprehensive and complete he is.

Verse 7: But among the Israelites not a dog will bark at any person or animal.' Then you will know that the Lord makes a distinction between Egypt and Israel.

God made a distinction again between Egypt and Israelites. Among the Hebrews, there was so much peace that not even a dog would bark at people or other animals. Imagine how often we hear dogs at night barking to ward off predators or as a warning. In this plague, God breathed complete peace and quiet over the Hebrew homes.

Verse 8: All these officials of yours will come to me, bowing down before me and saying, 'Go, you and all the people who follow you!'

After that I will leave." Then Moses, hot with anger, left Pharaoh.

Moses declared what is going to happen on his own terms this time. And when he left, he left with Pharaoh's officials bowing to him instead of Pharaoh, and he left with the officials' request for him to leave, not with an order by Pharaoh. Moses claimed God's authority but also claimed his authority over Pharaoh, apparently revealing his anger toward Pharaoh.

Reflection:

1. What is the significance of the firstborn? In biblical history? In my family history?

2. When have I found peace with God? When has God passed through my heart? When have I felt such peace and protection from God in the middle of the night that I didn't even hear a dog bark?

3. Why does Moses burn hot with anger if he has been listening to God and delivering God's messages to Pharaoh all along? Is it righteous anger, or is it a small peek into Moses' character flaw that will reveal itself again in the wilderness.

4. When have I allowed anger to cause me to make decisions on my terms rather than God's terms?

5. What must God be thinking and feeling when he kills the firstborn sons? Was he thinking about what will happen to his firstborn son in Jesus' future? Does he know the heartache of death to the firstborn son at the time when he is causing this plague in Egypt?

6. How has Pharaoh's power diminished through the ten plagues? He goes from not letting them go to "forcing" them to go, both as self-serving decisions.

Response:

_____

_____

_____

_____

_____

_____

_____

_____

_____

_____

_____

_____

DAY**12**

Exodus
Chapter Twelve

Summary:

Verse 1-2: 1 The Lord said to Moses and Aaron in Egypt, 2 "This month is to be for you the first month, the first month of your year.

God changed the calendar around this event! (And people today think that Daylight Savings Time is a big change!)

Verse 5: The animals you choose must be year-old males without defect, and you may take them from the sheep or the goats.

No defects for a sacrifice to the Lord! Do not slight God!

Verse 7: Then they are to take some of the blood and put it on the sides and tops of the doorframes of the houses where they eat the lambs.

Verse 10: Do not leave any of it till morning; if some is left till morning, you must burn it.

Passover meal - don't leave any for the next day - eat it or burn the leftovers.

Verse 11: This is how you are to eat it: with your cloak tucked into your belt, your sandals on your feet and your staff in your hand. Eat it in haste; it is the Lord's Passover.

Be ready always.

This was to be done every year and is law for all time.

1. Be fully dressed.
2. Wear sandals.
3. Carry a walking stick.

4. Eat with urgency.

5. Spread blood of the lamb on doorposts.

Verse 12:"On that same night I will pass through Egypt and strike down every firstborn of both people and animals, and I will bring judgment on all the gods of Egypt. I am the Lord.

God did not just declare judgment on Pharaoh and all the people of Egypt, but on ALL the gods of Egypt. He struck the death blow to every god that people worshiped for healing and long life.

Verse 14: "This is a day you are to commemorate; for the generations to come you shall celebrate it as a festival to the Lord—a lasting ordinance.

This was a day to remember...This is a law for all time. God commanded that he be remembered as their Savior!

Verse 15: For seven days you are to eat bread made without yeast. On the first day remove the yeast from your houses, for whoever eats anything with yeast in it from the first day through the seventh must be cut off from Israel.

Verse 16: On the first day hold a sacred assembly, and another one on the seventh day. Do no work at all on these days, except to prepare food for everyone to eat; that is all you may do.

God called a Sabbath for all time, not just in the Ten Commandments, but in the celebratory feasts.

Verse 19: For seven days no yeast is to be found in your houses. And anyone, whether foreigner or native-born, who eats anything with yeast in it must be cut off from the community of Israel.

The law applied to foreigners and native-born Israelites.

Verse 27: then tell them, 'It is the Passover sacrifice to the Lord, who passed over the houses of the Israelites in Egypt and spared our homes when he struck down the Egyptians.'" Then the people bowed down and worshiped.

All people bowed and worshiped at the news of the Passover feast.

Verse 29: At midnight the Lord struck down all the firstborn in Egypt, from the firstborn of Pharaoh, who sat on the throne, to the firstborn of the prisoner, who was in the dungeon, and the firstborn of all the livestock as well.

All the people paid the consequences for sin. Today we need to pray that we do not receive the consequences for the sins of our people and country.

Verse 31: During the night Pharaoh summoned Moses and Aaron and said, "Up! Leave my people, you and the Israelites! Go, worship the Lord as you have requested.

Pharaoh urgently sent for Moses and Aaron during the night. Imagine the mixed emotional message here: "Get out!...Go, but bless me as you leave." All Egyptians urged them to do so for fear of ALL dying. Pharaoh still wanted a blessing after all his refusals to allow them to leave. 600,000 men left Egypt (and women and children).

Verse 36: The Lord had made the Egyptians favorably disposed toward the people, and they gave them what they asked for; so they plundered the Egyptians.

Egyptians gave the Israelites whatever they asked for, either because the Egyptians favored them or because they were afraid of them and their God and wanted them to leave their country. The word "plunder" denotes an action that results in victory after a battle or war. God went to war for the Israelites and against the Egyptian gods and had victory. The Israelites did not have to strike a blow. They just needed to obey God's commands through the Passover. Yes, the Egyptians gave them what they asked for, and they demanded it all!

Verse 41: At the end of the 430 years, to the very day, all the Lord's divisions left Egypt.

After 430 years in Egypt, the Israelites left, moving toward their Promised Land, more than likely with mixed emotions with freedom from bondage but leaving what they knew to the unknown. This was definitely an epic "walk of faith"!

Verse 42: Because the Lord kept vigil that night to bring them out of Egypt, on this night all the Israelites are to keep vigil to honor the Lord for the generations to come.

Verse 48: "A foreigner residing among you who wants to celebrate the Lord's Passover must have all the males in his household circumcised; then he may take part like one born in the land. No uncircumcised male may eat it.

Everyone male had to have "skin in the game" (literally!) to be a part of the Lord's people and redemption.

Recap of Plagues

1. Blood - a blood covenant with God is complete and full.
2. Frogs - not man's timing, but God's timing. No relief/no recanting.
3. Gnats - even pagans testify of God's power.

4. Flies - God has power over territories, not just people.

5. Livestock - God sets the time. God affects property

6. Boils - God can act with no warning. God can affect physical bodies inside and out

7. Hail - God withholds judgment for his purpose - to show his power, to spread his fame

8. Locusts - God desires his story to be told through all generations

9. Darkness - God provides light for his people in a dark world

10. Death of Firstborn - God makes a distinction between the world and his people completely. God gives life, preserves life, and takes away life.

Plagues Connected with Egyptian gods: (https://pasoroblespress. com/commentary/gods-supremacy-over-the-false-gods-of-egypt-displayed-thru-the-10-plagues-by-dr-gary-barker/).

1. The water of the Nile was turned to Blood: Exodus 7:14-25. The gods judged: Hapi: the God of annual flooding; Osirus: The Nile River was his bloodstream.

2. Frogs: Exodus 8:1-15. The gods judged: Hapi and Hegt who had the head of a frog and were related to fertility: Hegt was a goddess.

3. Lice: These were tiny, stinging, blood sucking gnats. Exodus 8:16 -18. The God judged: Seb: the earth god.

4. Flies that came in swarms: Exodus 8:20-32. The gods judged: Hathor: the goddess of protection; Vatchi: fly God.

5. Livestock die: Exodus 9:1-7. The God judged: Apis: the bull god.

6. Boils on the body: Exodus 9:8-12. The God judged: Sekhmet: goddess of epidemics.

7. Hail and Fire: Exodus 9:13-15. The gods judged: Nut; the

sky goddess; Seth: God of storms; Shu: God of the atmosphere.

8. Locusts: Exodus 10:1-20. The gods judged: Siris: God of crops; Serapia: protector of crops.

9. Darkness: Exodus 10:21-29. The God judged: Ra: the sun god who was the most worshiped God in Egypt.

10. Death of the First Born: Exodus 11:1-12:36. The God judged: Heget: goddess of birth; Min; the God of reproduction. Deliverance from death was only through the offering of the Passover lamb. As a result of the plagues both Pharaoh and the Egyptians beg Moses and Israel to leave Egypt. God fulfilled His promise to free Israel.

Reflection:

1. God changed the calendar to revolve around the Passover. What events in my spiritual life mark new beginnings or milestones that I celebrate or think about every year?

2. How do we celebrate Passover today? (See chapter 13 where every firstborn is dedicated!) Do I still celebrate Passover today? Why or why not?

3. When I think about my own home, do I take steps to protect my home and family members by anointing my door frames with oil and prayer to proclaim God's protection over us? Do I do this symbolically or physically or both? Why is this important to me? From whom or what do I think I am guarding my home?

4. How are the directions for the Passover meal relevant to how we are to live our lives today?

5. The animals chosen for the Passover were to be without defects. This is a precursor to Jesus Christ as the Sacrificial Lamb without defects. When I offer my gifts, tithes, offerings, talents, time, etc. to God, how important is my efforts to make them without defects, pure and holy given unto the Lord?

6. The people had to fully rely on God for the next day's meal. Do I have enough faith to rely on God without hoarding my wealth, my food, my material goods?

7. How do I and my family commemorate all that God has done for me/us?

8. Is there any trace of worldly "yeast" in my home or at my job that compromises my promise to follow God and all of his promises? Where is my Achilles' heel for the enemy to break in, steal, and destroy?

9. Do I know anyone who believes in Jesus but rejects the Christian life, only asking for my blessing or advice or friendship? What can I do to move them closer to their Promised Land and total submission to God?

10. What gods or idols keep me from a close relationship with God? Which gods or idols need to be removed from my life?

11. What am I willing to do to get to my Promised Land? How long am I willing to wait?

12. Have I ever kept vigil to honor the Lord for all that he has done to deliver me?

Response:

_____

_____

_____

_____

_____

_____

_____

_____

_____

_____

_____

_____

_____

DAY**13**

Exodus
Chapter Thirteen

Summary:

Verses 1-2: 1 The Lord said to Moses, 2 "Consecrate to me every firstborn male. The first offspring of every womb among the Israelites belongs to me, whether human or animal."

Verse 7: Eat unleavened bread during those seven days; nothing with yeast in it is to be seen among you, nor shall any yeast be seen anywhere within your borders.

No yeast bread or any yeast is to be within the land.

Verse 8: On that day tell your son, 'I do this because of what the Lord did for me when I came out of Egypt.'

From this, it seems that God commands us to tell our children through generations what the Lord has done for us. Parents are the primary teacher of God's word and Biblical history. We are not to delegate all the responsibility to pastors and church leaders.

Verse 13: Redeem with a lamb every firstborn donkey, but if you do not redeem it, break its neck. Redeem every firstborn among your sons.

Verse 14-16: 14 "In days to come, when your son asks you, 'What does this mean?' say to him, 'With a mighty hand the Lord brought us out of Egypt, out of the land of slavery. 15 When Pharaoh stubbornly refused to let us go, the Lord killed the firstborn of both people and animals in Egypt. This is why I sacrifice to the Lord the first male offspring of every womb and redeem each of my firstborn sons.' 16 And it will be like a sign on your hand and a symbol on your forehead that the Lord brought us out of Egypt with his mighty hand."

Moses said that the people are to tell their children (their sons) about the mighty hand of the Lord delivering them out of Egypt and why they sacrifice lambs in memory of their redemption. Fast forward to 40 years in the wilderness where the people complained, rebelled, and betrayed God again and again. They (we as well) earned the description by God as being "a stiff-necked people." Thinking verse 13 metaphorically, people are the donkeys that God must redeem or break their necks. God sent his firstborn son, the Messiah Jesus, as the Lamb whose blood was shed once and for all for the forgiveness of their sins. For the "donkeys" who refuse to be redeemed, well, a stiff-neck becomes a broken neck resulting in death.

Verse 17: When Pharaoh let the people go, God did not lead them on the road through the Philistine country, though that was shorter. For God said, "If they face war, they might change their minds and return to Egypt.".

Verse 19: Moses took the bones of Joseph with him because Joseph had made the Israelites swear an oath. He had said, "God will surely come to your aid, and then you must carry my bones up with you from this place."

Moses carried Joseph's bones with him as he had promised. Even Joseph (posthumously) is delivered out of the land of slavery with his family to the Promised Land.

Verse 20: By day the Lord went ahead of them in a pillar of cloud to guide them on their way and by night in a pillar of fire to give them light, so that they could travel by day or night.

Verse 21: Neither the pillar of cloud by day nor the pillar of fire by night left its place in front of the people.

Whenever the people may have lost faith or doubted that the Lord was with them, they only needed to look at the pillar of cloud or fire to see his physical presence before them, guiding them.

Reflection:

1. Have I dedicated my firstborn to the Lord? Have I dedicated all my children and grandchildren to the Lord?

2. Is there any "yeast" in my life that still needs to be discarded or forbidden within my house, my family, my mind, my lifestyle, my actions?

3. How does the practice of buying the firstborn sons back relate to Jesus as God's One and Only son? How did God dedicate his firstborn and then buy him back?

4. Has God ever had to lead me in a roundabout way so that I wouldn't change my mind about something that I was called to do?

5. Has God ever led me along the longer path through a wilderness toward my Promised Land? If so, why?

6. Instead of a cloud by day and fire by night, how does God lead me so that I can keep moving forward in my spiritual journey?

7. What/who is my pillar by day/by night?

Response:

_____

_____

_____

_____

_____

_____

_____

_____

_____

_____

_____

_____

_____

_____

DAY**14**

Exodus
Chapter Fourteen

Summary:

Verse 1: Then the Lord said to Moses, 2 "Tell the Israelites to turn back and encamp near Pi Hahiroth, between Migdol and the sea. They are to encamp by the sea, directly opposite Baal Zephon. 3 Pharaoh will think, 'The Israelites are wandering around the land in confusion, hemmed in by the desert.'

Verse 5: When the king of Egypt was told that the people had fled, Pharaoh and his officials changed their minds about them and said, "What have we done? We have let the Israelites go and have lost their services!"

Verse 10: As Pharaoh approached, the Israelites looked up, and there were the Egyptians, marching after them. They were terrified and cried out to the Lord.

Verse 12: Didn't we say to you in Egypt, 'Leave us alone; let us serve the Egyptians'? It would have been better for us to serve the Egyptians than to die in the desert!"

People protested - "better to be a slave in Egypt than a corpse in the desert."

Verse 13-14: 13 Moses answered the people, "Do not be afraid. Stand firm and you will see the deliverance the Lord will bring you today. The Egyptians you see today you will never see again. 14 The Lord will fight for you; you need only to be still."

Life Advice from this verse:

1. Don't be afraid.
2. Stand firm.
3. Watch the Lord rescue you today.
4. The enemy (Egyptians) you see today will never be seen

again. Your cause of fear and struggle will disappear with God's help.

5. The Lord Himself will fight for you.

6. Stay calm.

Verse 15: Then the Lord said to Moses, "Why are you crying out to me? Tell the Israelites to move on.

Verse 16: Raise your staff and stretch out your hand over the sea to divide the water so that the Israelites can go through the sea on dry ground.

God told Moses to mobilize the people and to take action as their leader.

Verse 17: I will harden the hearts of the Egyptians so that they will go in after them. And I will gain glory through Pharaoh and all his army, through his chariots and his horsemen.

While Moses and the people were doing their part, God did his part by hardening the hearts of the enemy for their destruction; and God gets the glory.

Verse 19-20: 19 Then the angel of God, who had been traveling in front of Israel's army, withdrew and went behind them. The pillar of cloud also moved from in front and stood behind them, 20 coming between the armies of Egypt and Israel. Throughout the night the cloud brought darkness to the one side and light to the other side; so neither went near the other all night long.

The angel moved from front to rear between the Israelites and the Egyptians.

Verse 21: Then Moses stretched out his hand over the sea, and all that night the Lord drove the sea back with a strong east wind and turned it into dry land. The waters were divided,

Path through water - wind blew all night to dry land.

Verse 24: During the last watch of the night the Lord looked down from the pillar of fire and cloud at the Egyptian army and threw it into confusion.

Verse 29: But the Israelites went through the sea on dry ground, with a wall of water on their right and on their left.

Verse 30: That day the Lord saved Israel from the hands of the Egyptians, and Israel saw the Egyptians lying dead on the shore.

Verse 31: And when the Israelites saw the mighty hand of the Lord displayed against the Egyptians, the people feared the Lord and put their trust in him and in Moses his servant.

Life can be hard. Change is difficult. Sometimes we settle for less because we don't like change and perhaps fear the future. Sometimes things may get worse before getting better. When we trust God, he will make a way, "even when there seems to be no way."

Reflection:

1. When have I had to just stand still and stay calm to let God fight my battles for me?

2. Has God ever asked me to back up to move forward in battle?

3. When have I been "filled with awe" when God has moved in my life?

4. When has God asked me to move first before he can give me the victory and receive the glory?

5. When have I forgotten that God has destroyed the enemies of my past (fear, sin, doubt, oppression, trauma)?

Response:

_____

_____

_____

_____

_____

_____

_____

_____

_____

_____

DAY**15**

Exodus
Chapter Fifteen

Summary:

Verse 1: Then Moses and the Israelites sang this song to the Lord:

> *"I will sing to the Lord,*
> *for he is highly exalted.*
> *Both horse and driver*
> *he has hurled into the sea.*

The people remembered their victory in a song of praise.

Verse 20: Then Miriam the prophet, Aaron's sister, took a timbrel in her hand, and all the women followed her, with timbrels and dancing.

Verse 22-24: 22 Then Moses led Israel from the Red Sea and they went into the Desert of Shur. For three days they traveled in the desert without finding water. 23 When they came to Marah, they could not drink its water because it was bitter. (That is why the place is called Marah.) 24 So the people grumbled against Moses, saying, "What are we to drink?"

From the praises for the miracle of the Red Sea to thirst and complaints about thirst in the desert, it took just three days for the people to forget that God is God who provides.

Verse 25: Then Moses cried out to the Lord, and the Lord showed him a piece of wood. He threw it into the water, and the water became fit to drink.

The piece of wood turned bitter water clean, which could serve as another metaphor for God being the Water of Life saving his people using part of a tree.

Verse 26: He said, "If you listen carefully to the Lord your God and do what is right in his eyes, if you pay attention to his commands and keep all his decrees, I will not bring on you any of the diseases I brought on the Egyptians, for I am the Lord, who heals you."

Verse 27: Then they came to Elim, where there were twelve springs and seventy palm trees, and they camped there near the water.

Oasis of Elim = 12 springs and 70 palm trees, again water of life and the cover of trees.

Reflection:

1. How do praise songs help me and our children and grandchildren?

2. What is my favorite praise song? Why?

3. Right after a miracle comes a test of faith. What is/was mine?

4. What examples do I have that demonstrate verse 26 to be true?

5. If I wrote a Song of Deliverance for my life, what would the verses sound like? What would the melody sound like?

Response:

_____

_____

_____

DAY**16**

Exodus
Chapter Sixteen

Summary:

Verse 2: Just one month later, the people complain.

Verse 3: The Israelites said to them, "If only we had died by the Lord's hand in Egypt! There we sat around pots of meat and ate all the food we wanted, but you have brought us out into this desert to starve this entire assembly to death."

They glamorized their former life in slavery. This is not the description found in earlier verses of their conditions of life.

Verse 4: Then the Lord said to Moses, "I will rain down bread from heaven for you. The people are to go out each day and gather enough for that day. In this way I will test them and see whether they will follow my instructions.

God provided food, but just enough for each day as a test of their obedience.

Verse 8: Moses also said, "You will know that it was the Lord when he gives you meat to eat in the evening and all the bread you want in the morning, because he has heard your grumbling against him. Who are we? You are not grumbling against us, but against the Lord."

Verse 10: While Aaron was speaking to the whole Israelite community, they looked toward the desert, and there was the glory of the Lord appearing in the cloud.

Verse 19-20: 19 Then Moses said to them, "No one is to keep any of it until morning." 20 However, some of them paid no attention to Moses; they kept part of it until morning, but it was full of maggots and began to smell. So Moses was angry with them.

Some gathered a little; some a lot; each family had just what it needed. Those who saved it got maggots, lice, and stench. This is no different than today when there is a shortage of food; people hoard toilet paper and baby food to the detriment of others getting what they need. On the sixth day, the Israelites were to gather twice as much for the Sabbath (bake or boil and set aside)

Verse 27: Nevertheless, some of the people went out on the seventh day to gather it, but they found none.

Some people didn't trust God; they did not obey his commands. They had to test the conditions for themselves, which frustrated the Lord.

Verse 28-30: 28 Then the Lord said to Moses, "How long will you refuse to keep my commands and my instructions? 29 Bear in mind that the Lord has given you the Sabbath; that is why on the sixth day he gives you bread for two days. Everyone is to stay where they are on the seventh day; no one is to go out." 30 So the people rested on the seventh day.

The Sabbath was given to the people as a gift. A day of rest on the seventh day was a blessing. Manna, white like coriander seed and tasting like honey wafers, was their daily provision of food that they did not have to harvest. The provision of manna as daily sustenance is such a powerful act of God, not with lightning and thunder, but with soft flakes of a bread like substance falling from the sky to the ground, from God to his people. This was his daily act of love. They would not have to hunt for food; they could sleep at night expecting that God would provide in the morning. There is no other manna miracle in Scripture that is as concrete: they could see it, hold it, taste it, swallow it as their bread of life. When we read that Jesus told his disciples that he is the bread of life, how could they not have thought about the Manna God of their people, the manna preserved in the ark of the covenant. When I doubt that God will provide, I must remember my Manna God and Jesus, the bread of life.

Verse 32: Moses said, "This is what the Lord has commanded: 'Take an omer of manna and keep it for the generations to come, so they can see the bread I gave you to eat in the wilderness when I brought you out of Egypt.'"

A 2-quart container was filled and saved to show future generations. It was to be kept in the Ark of the Covenant. How awesome it would be for someone to discover the Ark of the Covenant today and find the container of manna preserved for generations to come!

Verse 35: The Israelites ate manna for forty years, until they came to a land that was settled; they ate manna until they reached the border of Canaan

Reflection:

1. How do we honor the gift of the Sabbath?

2. The Israelites ate the same food (manna) for 40 years. Do I complain about leftovers or eating the same food that I had yesterday?

3. What makes people continually disobey God, even when they have been given specific instructions? Yet God shows us mercy.

Response:

_____

_____

_____

DAY**17**

Exodus
Chapter Seventeen

Summary:

Water from the Rock - People were ready to stone Moses because of thirst. Moses used the same staff that struck the Nile River turning to blood for Egypt for the staff to bring forth clean water for Israelites. Instead of the people using rocks to harm Moses, God used the rock at Mount Sinai to give water to the people through Moses.

Verse 3: But the people were thirsty for water there, and they grumbled against Moses. They said, "Why did you bring us up out of Egypt to make us and our children and livestock die of thirst?"

As a leader, Moses must have been hurt by these personal accusations, as if he would intentionally want to cause the death of his people, including children.

Verse 4: Then Moses cried out to the Lord, "What am I to do with these people? They are almost ready to stone me."

Verse 5: The Lord answered Moses, "Go out in front of the people. Take with you some of the elders of Israel and take in your hand the staff with which you struck the Nile, and go.

Verse 6: I will stand there before you by the rock at Horeb. Strike the rock, and water will come out of it for the people to drink." So Moses did this in the sight of the elders of Israel.

Moses struck the rock as he was told, and water gushed out as the elders looked on.

Verse 7: And he called the place Massah and Meribah because the Israelites quarreled and because they tested the Lord saying, "Is the Lord among us or not?"

Moses named the place Massah (which means "test") and Meribah (which means "arguing").

Verse 9: Moses said to Joshua, "Choose some of our men and go out to fight the Amalekites. Tomorrow I will stand on top of the hill with the staff of God in my hands."

This is the second time that Moses' staff is referred to as "the staff of God", thus, signifying that the authority and power demonstrated by Moses was that of God, not of man.

Verse 10-13: 10 So Joshua fought the Amalekites as Moses had ordered, and Moses, Aaron and Hur went to the top of the hill. 11 As long as Moses held up his hands, the Israelites were winning, but whenever he lowered his hands, the Amalekites were winning. 12 When Moses' hands grew tired, they took a stone and put it under him and he sat on it. Aaron and Hur held his hands up—one on one side, one on the other—so that his hands remained steady till sunset. 13 So Joshua overcame the Amalekite army with the sword.

Verse 14: Then the Lord said to Moses, "Write this on a scroll as something to be remembered and make sure that Joshua hears it, because I will completely blot out the name of Amalek from under heaven."

Verse 15: Moses built an altar and called it The Lord is my Banner

Reflection:

1. God makes the impossible possible. When has that happened to me? What am I asking God for now that some would say is impossible?

2. What terrible names would places be called if they were

named from the attitudes and actions of my own?

3. Who holds my hands up and gives me rest during a spiritual battle?

4. What altar could I build as a remembrance of "The Lord is my banner"?

5. What do I need to write down for my future generations about God's power and movement in my life?

6. Rocks were used to stone people to death and to quench the people's thirst. What in my life has been used for both destructive and constructive purposes?

Response:

_____

_____

_____

_____

_____

_____

_____

_____

DAY**18**

Exodus
Chapter Eighteen

Summary:

Father-in-law Jethro visits Moses camped near the mountain of God.

Verse 2-4: 2 After Moses had sent away his wife Zipporah, his father-in-law Jethro received her 3 and her two sons. One son was named Gershom,for Moses said, "I have become a foreigner in a foreign land"; 4 and the other was named Eliezer, for he said, "My father's God was my helper; he saved me from the sword of Pharaoh."Moses had sent Zipporah and their two sons back to his father-in-law.

Verse 6: Jethro had sent word to him, "I, your father-in-law Jethro, am coming to you with your wife and her two sons."

Father-in-law Jethro returns with them to Moses. The text doesn't say how long Grandpa Jethro had to babysit the grandsons, but what grandparent hasn't been ready to take their grandchildren back to their parents after an extended time of care? Jethro also must have known that husband, wife, and children needed to be together.

Verse 12: Then Jethro, Moses' father-in-law, brought a burnt offering and other sacrifices to God, and Aaron came with all the elders of Israel to eat a meal with Moses' father-in-law in the presence of God.

Verse 14: When his father-in-law saw all that Moses was doing for the people, he said, "What is this you are doing for the people? Why do you alone sit as judge, while all these people stand around you from morning till evening?"

Verse 15: Moses answered him, "Because the people come to me to seek God's will.

Verse 16: ...(Moses) Whenever they have a dispute, it is brought to me, and I decide between the parties and inform them of God's decrees and instructions."

Verse 18: ...(Jethro) You and these people who come to you will only wear yourselves out. The work is too heavy for you; you cannot handle it alone.

Verse 21: But select capable men from all the people—men who fear God, trustworthy men who hate dishonest gain—and appoint them as officials over thousands, hundreds, fifties and tens.

Verse 22: Have them serve as judges for the people at all times, but have them bring every difficult case to you; the simple cases they can decide themselves. That will make your load lighter, because they will share it with you.

Reflection:

1. When have I tried to accomplish a task all alone without asking for help?

2. Am I open to listening to wise counsel from other godly people, including my family and in-laws?

3. How do I choose my closest confidants and helpers/ partners? Are they capable and honest and fear God and hate bribes?

4. Who is someone in my life who has saved me from myself, who has supported me in my spiritual walk?

5. What do I do to endure the pressures of life and leadership?

Response:

DAY**19**

Exodus
Chapter Nineteen

Summary:

Verse 1: On the first day of the third month after the Israelites left Egypt—on that very day—they came to the Desert of Sinai.

After two months exactly from leaving Egypt, the Israelites arrived at Mount Sinai's base.

Verse 2: After they set out from Rephidim, they entered the Desert of Sinai, and Israel camped there in the desert in front of the mountain.

Verses 3-6: 3 Then Moses went up to God, and the Lord called to him from the mountain and said, "This is what you are to say to the descendants of Jacob and what you are to tell the people of Israel: 4 'You yourselves have seen what I did to Egypt, and how I carried you on eagles' wings and brought you to myself. 5 Now if you obey me fully and keep my covenant, then out of all nations you will be my treasured possession. Although the whole earth is mine, 6 you will be for me a kingdom of priests and a holy nation.' These are the words you are to speak to the Israelites."

Moses climbed the mountain to appear before God (from appearing before Pharaoh to now appearing before God)

Verse 8: The people all responded together, "We will do everything the Lord has said." So Moses brought their answer back to the Lord.

Verse 9: The Lord said to Moses, "I am going to come to you in a dense cloud, so that the people will hear me speaking with you and will always put their trust in you." Then Moses told the Lord what the people had said.

Verse 10: Boundaries were set and consecration was commanded.

The penalty for disobedience is death. The people were to wash, abstain from sex, and wait three days.

Verse 12-13: 12 Put limits for the people around the mountain and tell them, 'Be careful that you do not approach the mountain or touch the foot of it. Whoever touches the mountain is to be put to death. 13 They are to be stoned or shot with arrows; not a hand is to be laid on them. No person or animal shall be permitted to live.' Only when the ram's horn sounds a long blast may they approach the mountain."

Verse 16: lightning, thunder, dense cloud, ram's horn

Verse 18-19: 18 Mount Sinai was covered with smoke, because the Lord descended on it in fire. The smoke billowed up from it like smoke from a furnace, and the whole mountain trembled violently. 19 As the sound of the trumpet grew louder and louder, Moses spoke and the voice of God answered him.

The people would recognize smoke from a furnace or kiln because of their brick-making days in slavery to Egypt. Moses had gone from meeting God in a burning bush to meeting God on a burning mountain!

Verse 23: Moses said to the Lord, "The people cannot come up Mount Sinai, because you yourself warned us, 'Put limits around the mountain and set it apart as holy.'"

Moses protested God's warning to the people, "You already warned us." These stubborn people probably needed more than one warning.

Verse 24: The Lord replied, "Go down and bring Aaron up with you. But the priests and the people must not force their way through to come up to the Lord, or he will break out against them."

"Bring Aaron." God called for Aaron to come back with Moses. What an honor! And how frightening at the same time!

Reflection:

1. What's the difference between Moses in front of Pharaoh and in front of God?

2. When has just two months made all the difference in my physical or spiritual life?

3. When have I protested to God about my life or his guidance?

4. Who has God sent to help me in my spiritual journey? Who lifts me up when I am weary in leadership or in my job?

5. Do I feel like I am God's own special treasure, God's kingdom of praise, God's holy nation? What can I do to further obey his commands in order to live in this unique and elevated relationship with God?

Response:

_____

_____

_____

_____

_____

_____

_____

_____

_____

_____

DAY**20**

Exodus
Chapter Twenty

Summary:

The Ten Commandments

Verse 5: I lay the sins of the parents upon their children. The entire family is affected, even children in the third and fourth generations of those who reject me.

Verse 6: But I lavish unfailing love for a thousand generations on those who love me and obey my commands.

Verse 12: Honor your father and mother. Then you will live a full life in the land the Lord your God is giving you.

Verse 18-19: 18 When the people saw the thunder and lightning and heard the trumpet and saw the mountain in smoke, they trembled with fear. They stayed at a distance 19 and said to Moses, "Speak to us yourself and we will listen. But do not have God speak to us or we will die."

The people showed a real fear of God and felt unworthy of hearing God's voice for themselves. They asked Moses to be the intermediary.

Verse 20: Moses said to the people, "Do not be afraid. God has come to test you, so that the fear of God will be with you to keep you from sinning."

Verse 23: No idols of silver or gold

Verse 24-25: 24 "'Make an altar of earth for me and sacrifice on it your burnt offerings and fellowship offerings, your sheep and goats and your cattle. Wherever I cause my name to be honored, I will come to you and bless you. 25 If you make an altar of stones for me, do not build it with dressed stones, for you will defile it if you use a tool on it.

Altar - only material was stones and no steps..

Reflection:

1. What sin in my family is generational?
2. What unfailing love in our family is generational?
3. When have I been fearful of God's power? In awe of what God has done?
4. Where and when could I build an altar?
5. When has God spoken to me or through a prophet to me?

Response:

_____

_____

_____

_____

_____

_____

_____

_____

_____

_____

_____

_____

DAY**21**

Exodus
Chapter Twenty-One

Summary:

Verses 1-11: laws for slaves to be free

Verse 12: justice for murderers, kidnappers, dishonor of parents, compensation for injury to others (slaves considered property)

Verse 15: assault and kill = death; kidnapper = death; dishonor parents = death

Verse 19: compensation

Verse 21: slave is property

Verse 23: life for a life, eye for an eye, tooth for a tooth, a hand for a hand, a foot for a foot, a burn for a burn, a wound for a wound, a bruise for a bruise (punishment fits the crime/injury)

Verse 30: The owner of the ox may redeem his life by paying whatever is demanded.

Verse 32: If the bull gores a male or female slave, the owner must pay thirty shekels of silver to the master of the slave, and the bull is to be stoned to death.

"30 silver coins" payment for an ox goring a slave, male or female. In Matthew 26.15, thirty pieces of silver were paid to Judas for Jesus. The price for betraying Jesus was the same as the price for a slave, perhaps signifying Jesus' continued portrayal of being a servant to man.

Old Testament judgment is to be overturned by Jesus in the New Testament.

Reflection:

1. For what groups does God demand justice?

2. How does God use the term "redeem" in this chapter?

3. Meditate on verse 31 with the 30 silver coins. Where do we read about 30 pieces of silver in the New Testament?

4. Why is God's instructions of "life for life, eye for eye" no longer valid for Christians today?

Response:

_____

_____

_____

_____

_____

_____

_____

_____

_____

_____

_____

DAY**22**

Exodus
Chapter Twenty-Two

Summary:

Protection of property; judges (or God) settles disputes; seduction of a virgin.

Verse 18: A sorceress should not be permitted to live.

Verse 19: Sodomy (sex with animals) = death

Verse 20: sacrifice to other gods = death

Verse 21: do not mistreat foreigners

Verse 22: do not exploit widows or orphans; personal to God

Verse 24: I (God) will kill you with a sword

Verse 28: Do not dishonor God or curse your rulers. Give me your firstborn sons, cattle, sheep, and goats.

Verse 31: You must be my holy people. (Call to holiness.).

Reflection:

1. Why is God so against sorcery and sodomy that the punishment is death?
2. Do I welcome foreigners and treat them with respect?
3. Do I curse my/our rulers?
4. How can I/we become the "holy people" that God orders me/us to be?

Response:

_____

_____

_____

_____

_____

_____

_____

_____

_____

_____

DAY**23**

Exodus
Chapter Twenty-Three

Summary:

Verse 1: no lying

Verse 5: stop and help neighbors

Verse 6: don't deny justice to the poor

Verse 8: no bribes - it twists truth

Verse 9: do not oppress foreigners

Verse 10: plant and harvest crops for 6 years - rest the 7th. Let the poor harvest whatever grows on its own.

Verse 12: Rest on 7th day - rest and recharge

Verse 14: Three Festivals:

    a. Unleavened Bread - departure from Egypt

    b. Harvest - bring me first of crops

    c. Final Harvest - bring the very best of the first harvest to the house of the Lord your God

Verse 20: God sent an angel for protection

Verse 23: Utterly destroy their gods and their sacred pillars

Verse 25: Serve only the Lord your God...and I will give you full, long lives.

Verse 27: "my terror" - God can create panic, drive out enemies, not all at once, because wild animals would multiply and threaten you.

Verse 30: a little at a time until your population has increased. Boundaries are Red Sea to Mediterranean Sea, eastern wilderness to Euphrates.

Verse 32: No treaties with them or their gods. It will cause you to sin against me.

Reflection:

1. What does God ask me to remember or to celebrate?
2. What freedoms or liberties do I celebrate?
3. Do I bring God my very best of my "harvest"?
4. Do I serve only the Lord my God?
5. Do I follow the tenets set down by God in Exodus 23?

Response:

_____

_____

_____

_____

_____

_____

_____

_____

_____

_____

_____

_____

DAY**24**

Exodus
Chapter Twenty-Four

Summary:

74 people saw God!

Verse 1-2: 1 Then the Lord said to Moses, "Come up to the Lord, you and Aaron, Nadab and Abihu, and seventy of the elders of Israel. You are to worship at a distance, 2 but Moses alone is to approach the Lord; the others must not come near. And the people may not come up with him."

Verse 3: When Moses went and told the people all the Lord's words and laws, they responded with one voice, "Everything the Lord has said we will do."

Verse 4: Moses then wrote down everything the Lord had said. He got up early the next morning and built an altar at the foot of the mountain and set up twelve stone pillars representing the twelve tribes of Israel.

Verse 7: Then he took the Book of the Covenant and read it to the people. They responded, "We will do everything the Lord has said; we will obey."

Verse 9-11: 9 Moses and Aaron, Nadab and Abihu, and the seventy elders of Israel went up 10 and saw the God of Israel. Under his feet was something like a pavement made of lapis lazuli, as bright blue as the sky. 11 But God did not raise his hand against these leaders of the Israelites; they saw God, and they ate and drank.

Seventy-four people ate a covenant meal in God's presence (and did not die!) The Bible makes mention of times when God is seen by humans and also mentions that none has seen his face. God is so great that we cannot fully see him. Even so, what we can see is undeniably him.

Verse 12: The Lord said to Moses, "Come up to me on the mountain and stay here, and I will give you the tablets of stone with the law and commandments I have written for their instruction."

Tablets supplied by God. Inscription written by God.

Verse 13: Then Moses set out with Joshua his aide, and Moses went up on the mountain of God.

Moses and Joshua climbed the mountain for stone tablets inscribed by God. Aaron and Hur are left to supervise the rest of the elders.

Verse 15-16: When Moses went up on the mountain, the cloud covered it, 16 and the glory of the Lord settled on Mount Sinai. For six days the cloud covered the mountain, and on the seventh day the Lord called to Moses from within the cloud.

Verse 17: To the Israelites the glory of the Lord looked like a consuming fire on top of the mountain.

Verse 18: Then Moses entered the cloud as he went on up the mountain. And he stayed on the mountain forty days and forty nights.

Reflection:

1. When have I seen God? In communion or during a meal with others?

2. What are my pillars? Who are my pillars?

3. Why would it have been significant that the Lord provided the commandments?

4. Do I see God as a consuming fire in my life? Purified? Sanctified? All encompassing?

5. Have I ever spent 40 days and nights with God?

Response:

_____

_____

_____

_____

_____

_____

_____

_____

_____

_____

_____

_____

DAY**25**

Exodus
Chapter Twenty-Five

Summary:

Offerings for the Tabernacle. People of Israel - build a sanctuary so I can live among them. Ark of the Covenant contains stone tablets: a written contract "etched in stone"!

"I will talk to you from above the atonement cover." Bread of the Presence in the Ark of the Covenant.

Verse 2: "Tell the Israelites to bring me an offering. You are to receive the offering for me from everyone whose heart prompts them to give.

Verse 3-7: Special offerings:

Gold/silver, bronze

Blue, purple, scarlet thread

Fine linen/goat hair cloths

Tanned ram skin/fine goatskin leather

Acacia wood

Olive oil for lamps

Spices for anointing oil and the fragrant incense

Onyx stones/gemstones for the priest's ephods

Verse 8-9: 8 "Then have them make a sanctuary for me, and I will dwell among them. 9 Make this tabernacle and all its furnishings exactly like the pattern I will show you.

Verse 10: "Have them make an ark of acacia wood—two and a half cubits long, a cubit and a half wide, and a cubit and a half high.

Verse 21-22: 21 Place the cover on top of the ark and put in the ark the tablets of the covenant law that I will give you. 22 There, above the cover between the two cherubim that are over the ark of the covenant law, I will meet with you and give you all my commands for the Israelites.

Verse 30: Put the bread of the Presence on this table to be before me at all times

Reflection:

1. Why is it important that God wants offerings "from everyone whose heart prompts them to give"? Do I give my tithes and offerings to the Lord from my heart?

2. The Israelites left slavery with the gifts and treasures given to them by the Egyptians. Now God is asking for them to give him part of their treasures to build a tabernacle for the Lord. How difficult must it have been for the former slaves to give up their newfound wealth to build a tabernacle?

3. God says to make this tabernacle exactly like his pattern. Why would God be so specific in his instructions? Why wouldn't God let the craftsmen design something original from their imaginations and craftsmanship to honor the Lord?

4. Am I vigilant about following God's commands exactly, or am I tempted to inject my own ideas and designs to "express myself"?

Response:

_____

_____

_____

_____

_____

_____

_____

_____

_____

_____

_____

_____

_____

_____

DAY**26**

Exodus
Chapter Twenty-Six

Summary:

Plans for the tabernacle in detail.

God is a God of detailed instructions and expectations for his people. He planned his own place of meeting his people with the finest of the earth's materials and his people's craftsmanship.

Reflection:

1. Why was it important for God to have a tabernacle built from the finest of earth's materials and people's craftsmanship?

2. How does a place of worship affect my ability to worship, to pray, and to hear God?

3. People around the world worship in huge cathedrals, small adobe huts, open air fields, and tiny chapels. Where am I most comfortable worshiping and praying to God? Why?

4. Does my quality of worship change, depending upon my surroundings or physical structure? Does my quality of worship change, depending upon the people around me? The music around me?

Response:

_____

_____

_____

_____

DAY**27**

Exodus
Chapter Twenty-Seven

Summary:
Plans for the Altar of Burnt Offering, The Courtyard, and the Light for the Tabernacle.

Verse 20: "Command the Israelites to bring you clear oil of pressed olives for the light so that the lamps may be kept burning.

Verse 21: In the tent of meeting, outside the curtain that shields the ark of the covenant law, Aaron and his sons are to keep the lamps burning before the Lord from evening till morning. This is to be a lasting ordinance among the Israelites for the generations to come.

Reflection:

1. How is the requirement for pure oil consistent with God's other commands?

2. What is the significance of the lamps burning in the Lord's presence all night? What would that have meant to the Israelites and their descendants?

Response:

_____

_____

_____

_____

_____

_____

_____

_____

_____

_____

_____

_____

DAY**28**

Exodus
Chapter Twenty-Eight

Summary:
Priests' clothing.

Verse 1: "Have Aaron your brother brought to you from among the Israelites, along with his sons Nadab and Abihu, Eleazar and Ithamar, so they may serve me as priests.

Aaron, sons Nadah, Abihu, Eleazar, and Ithamar were set apart as priests with "glorious and beautiful" garments. Names of 12 tribes were on the stones.

Verse 12: and fasten them on the shoulder pieces of the ephod as memorial stones for the sons of Israel. Aaron is to bear the names on his shoulders as a memorial before the Lord.

Verse 15: "Fashion a breastpiece for making decisions—the work of skilled hands. Make it like the ephod: of gold, and of blue, purple and scarlet yarn, and of finely twisted linen.

Verse 29-30: "Whenever Aaron enters the Holy Place, he will bear the names of the sons of Israel over his heart on the breastpiece of decision as a continuing memorial before the Lord. 30 Also put the Urim and the Thummim in the breastpiece, so they may be over Aaron's heart whenever he enters the presence of the Lord. Thus Aaron will always bear the means of making decisions for the Israelites over his heart before the Lord.

The Urim and Thummim were gemstones or oracles used by the priests to determine God's will or revelation. The Hebrew translation is "those whose words are light" and "those whose words are fulfilled". (https://www.jewishencyclopedia.com/articles/14609-urim-and-thummim)

Verse 35: Aaron must wear it when he ministers. The sound of the bells will be heard when he enters the Holy Place before the Lord and when he comes out, so that he will not die.

Verse 41: Clothe, anoint, and ordain and consecrate Aaron and sons as permanent law.

Reflection:

1. In what ways do we continue to place priests/pastors in leadership with clothing, anointing, ordaining, and consecrating them?

2. Instead of the Urim and Thummim today, how do I determine the Lord's will for his people? How do I make decisions that are aligned with God's will for my life?

3. Why was it important for Aaron to bear the names of the sons of Israel over his heart?

4. Why was it important for Urim and Thummin to be over Aaron's heart whenever he entered the presence of the Lord?

5. How do I protect my heart for the Lord?

6. How do I prepare myself to be in the presence of the Lord?

Response:

_____

_____

_____

_____

DAY**29**

Exodus
Chapter Twenty-Nine

Summary:
Dedication of the Priests

> *Verse 20: Slaughter it, take some of its blood and put it on the lobes of the right ears of Aaron and his sons, on the thumbs of their right hands, and on the big toes of their right feet. Then splash blood against the sides of the altar.*

Aaron and his sons were to be ordained to hear the word of God (with their ears), to do the work of the Lord (with their hands), and to walk (toes) in the precepts of the Lord as a priesthood set apart for generations. The right side was considered the "right" side of honor, status, and strength.

Consider the servant to the high priest, Malchus, whose right ear was cut off by Simon Peter during the arrest of Jesus in the Garden of Gethsemane and restored by Jesus. The job of Malchus was to report back to the Jewish high priest, Caiaphas, what he had seen and heard. Since the Jewish high priest would have been ordained with ram's blood on his right ear, this action of his servant losing his right may have carried significance for Caiaphas. Was it a message from Jesus to the high priest? The Son of God, the Lamb of God, had been teaching in the temple, but the high priests "heard" and did not believe in him. Instead they accused him. Why did Jesus restore the servant's ear? Perhaps because Jesus wanted no shedding of blood other than his own for the redemption of sin; perhaps because Jesus wanted to show love not violence in his ministry; or perhaps because Jesus wanted to demonstrate that he was the Lamb of God being led to the slaughter for both his friends and enemies, Jews and Gentiles.

I would have loved to have heard the report of the servant when he returned to the Jewish high priest, Caiaphas. Perhaps he touched his right ear and winced about the thought of it, as well as his anointing, being cut off. In reality, the anointing of the Jewish priests had passed and a new great high priest, Jesus, was to take supreme authority over life and death through his resurrection.

> *Verse 42: "For the generations to come this burnt offering is to be made regularly at the entrance to the tent of meeting, before the Lord. There I will meet you and speak to you;*
>
> *Verse 43: there also I will meet with the Israelites, and the place will be consecrated by my glory.*
>
> *Verse 45-46: Then I will dwell among the Israelites and be their God. 46 They will know that I am the Lord their God, who brought them out of Egypt so that I might dwell among them. I am the Lord their God.*

Reflection:

1. How important is it for God to live among his people? To what extent has God gone to come close to us?

2. How do I respond to God, knowing how much he wants a relationship with me?

Response:

_____

_____

_____

_____

_____

_____

_____

_____

_____

_____

_____

Exodus
Chapter Thirty

Summary:
Plans for Incense Altar

Verse 6: Put the altar in front of the curtain that shields the ark of the covenant law—before the atonement cover that is over the tablets of the covenant law—where I will meet with you.

Verse 11-12: Then the Lord said to Moses, 12 "When you take a census of the Israelites to count them, each one must pay the Lord a ransom for his life at the time he is counted. Then no plague will come on them when you number them.

Each man (21 years old +) must pay a ransom for himself to the Lord - a small piece of silver. This is such a powerful tie back to the exodus and forward to the fulfillment.

Verse 21: Aaron and sons must always wash their hands and feet when going into the Tabernacle or they will die - permanent law

Verse 33: holy oil only for priests - salted, pure, and sacred

Verse 37: Do not make any incense with this formula for yourselves; consider it holy to the Lord.

Reflection:

1. We are part of the redeeming process to be with the Lord. How am I fulfilling my redemption in my life today?

2. Do I cleanse myself (physically and spiritually) before going before the Lord?

3. How do we use holy oil today?

Response:

DAY**31**

Exodus
Chapter Thirty-One

Summary:

Verse 1-4: God specifically chose an expert craftsman - Bezalel of the tribe of Judah and grandson of Hur, filled him with great wisdom, ability, expertise in all kinds of crafts

Verse 13: Keep the Sabbath as a sign of the covenant

Verse 15: Anyone working on the Sabbath = death - permanent sign

Verse 18: When the Lord finished speaking to Moses on Mount Sinai, he gave him the two tablets of the covenant law, the tablets of stone inscribed by the finger of God.

Reflection:

1. Has God chosen me for my specific skills or talents to do his work?
2. How do I honor the Sabbath today?

Response:

_____

_____

_____

_____

_____

_____

_____

_____

_____

_____

_____

_____

DAY**32**

Exodus
Chapter Thirty-Two

Summary:
Gold Calf

Verse 1: When the people saw that Moses was so long in coming down from the mountain, they gathered around Aaron and said, "Come, make us gods[a] who will go before us. As for this fellow Moses who brought us up out of Egypt, we don't know what has happened to him."

People would not wait, so they pressured Aaron to "make us some gods who can lead us." "This fellow Moses…" Wow!

Verse 2: Aaron answered them, "Take off the gold earrings that your wives, your sons and your daughters are wearing, and bring them to me."

The gold from them had come from Egypt, so pagan gold was then fired into a pagan god, the calf.

Verse 4: He took what they handed him and made it into an idol cast in the shape of a calf, fashioning it with a tool. Then they said, "These are your gods, Israel, who brought you up out of Egypt."

What short memories! So sad for God! No wonder that God emphasized retelling the truth to future generations!

Verse 5: When Aaron saw this, he built an altar in front of the calf and announced, "Tomorrow there will be a festival to the Lord."

Aaron built an idol but called a festival to the Lord. This was an example of combining their religious traditions with pagan traditions, which would be abhorrent to the Lord.

Verse 6: So the next day the people rose early and sacrificed burnt offerings and presented fellowship offerings. Afterward they sat down to eat and drink and got up to indulge in revelry.

Sacrifices to a golden calf? burnt offerings? pagan revelry? They didn't do this in Egypt, did they?

Verse 7: Then the Lord said to Moses, "Go down, because your people, whom you brought up out of Egypt, have become corrupt.

God said to Moses, "Quick! Go!" "How quickly they turned from me."

Verse 9-10: "I have seen these people," the Lord said to Moses, "and they are a stiff-necked people. 10 Now leave me alone so that my anger may burn against them and that I may destroy them. Then I will make you into a great nation."

God's fierce anger blazed against them to the point of wanting to destroy them and start over with Moses as a leader of a great nation.

Verse 12: Why should the Egyptians say, 'It was with evil intent that he brought them out, to kill them in the mountains and to wipe them off the face of the earth'? Turn from your fierce anger; relent and do not bring disaster on your people.

Moses pled again for mercy for the people and asked God to change his mind.

Verse 13: Remember your servants Abraham, Isaac and Israel, to whom you swore by your own self: 'I will make your descendants as numerous as the stars in the sky and I will give your descendants all this land I promised them, and it will be their inheritance forever.'"

Moses reminded God of his oath to Abraham, Isaac, and Jacob.

Verse 14: So the Lord changed his mind and showed mercy on the people.

Verse 17: Joshua heard sounds of war.

Verse 18: Moses heard sounds of celebration and turned to burn with anger upon seeing the people and the calf

  a. Smashed tablets

  b. Burnt calf

  c. Ground it into power

  d. Forced the people to drink it (oh, the bitter cup!)

Verse 21: He said to Aaron, "What did these people do to you, that you led them into such great sin?"

Verse 22-24: 22 "Do not be angry, my lord," Aaron answered. "You know how prone these people are to evil. 23 They said to me, 'Make us gods who will go before us. As for this fellow Moses who brought us up out of Egypt, we don't know what has happened to him.' 24 So I told them, 'Whoever has any gold jewelry, take it off.' Then they gave me the gold, and I threw it into the fire, and out came this calf!"

Aaron did not take responsibility for his leadership and his actions. He sounded childish as he explained that he just threw the gold in the fire, and out came a calf. Talk about leadership gone wrong!

With Moses, Aaron was present or participated when all the miracles happened in front of Pharaoh; he was ordained (set apart) to be a priest in chapter 20; Aaron and Hur were left to supervise the elders when Moses and Joshua went higher up on the mountain to receive the first set of commandments inscribed by God (24:13); and Aaron was dedicated with his sons as priests with blood anointing their rights ears, right thumbs, and right toes (29:20). It would appear that Aaron would have been ready and strong enough to supervise and lead the people by himself (without Moses, Hur, or his priestly sons). However, by this chapter 32, Moses had gone back up the mountain for the second set of commandments from God.

Acting alone, without another leader by his side for support, Aaron became distracted by the people and bowed to their pressure because he wanted to please them. He allowed himself to forget God's commands and to be convinced by the people to make a golden idol similar to idol worship images that they had left behind in Egypt. Called by God, ordained, anointed, and placed in leadership, Aaron failed as a Godly leader without the strong support from the absent but busy Moses. Aaron got sucked into the requests of the people and their bent toward the cultural influences of their old life in Egypt. He made the terrible decision to lead the people in idol worship, an act abhorrent to God, who commanded the people to make no graven images and to put God first in their lives. Aaron was so far into his leadership error that he blamed the people for his mistakes. However, our merciful and forgiving God, after doling out punishment for disobedience, allowed Aaron to lead his family of Levites as the priests to maintain God's temple. Aaron may not have been assigned to supervise the people by himself again, but he did continue his assignment as the priest of the temple.

If anyone ever feels as though God would never forgive them for the worst abhorrence against God, study the life of Aaron. God always desires a relationship with each person. Always. In 40:12, when the God's tabernacle is established, Aaron and his sons are washed, dressed, and anointed, set apart to do what they were called to do. As Aaron was being washed, purified,and anointed, perhaps he felt unworthy as he fought back thoughts of regrets about the calf incident. God put into place the rituals for him to remember his first calling: to serve God, and to serve God only.

Verse 25-27: 25 Moses saw that the people were running wild and that Aaron had let them get out of control and so become a laughingstock to their enemies. 26 So he stood at the entrance to the camp and said, "Whoever is for the Lord, come to me." And all the Levites rallied to him. 27 Then he said to them, "This is what the Lord, the God of Israel, says: 'Each man strap a sword to his side. Go back and forth through the camp from one end to the other, each killing his brother and friend and neighbor.'"

Moses called for those who are on his side: Levites gather around him. Moses commanded the Levites to kill all brothers, friends, and neighbors. Three thousand people died during this display of idol worship. (Since I am personalizing the Levites as my own family in this story, I am proud of the fact that all the Levites rallied to Moses in loyalty to God. The whole family stood ready to re-establish worship and order back to God. However, I am deeply disturbed by the thought of brothers having to kill brothers because of wild, anti-God behaviors). How awful for all of Israel to lose loved ones in this way: not from an enemy in another kingdom outside of Israel, but from within their own people. This must have taken great courage to obey God in this way.

Consider the difference between the murder of the Egyptian by Moses in Exodus 2:12 and the murders of the brothers by the Levites in Exodus 32:27. In Exodus 2, Moses took an Egyptian man's life into his own hands to defend a Hebrew slave, and when Moses questioned a Hebrew fighting a Hebrew, the one in the wrong asked, "Who made you ruler and judge over us?" Ironically, eventually Moses would become their ruler and judge. However, Moses was not in the position to be judge or ruler or executioner. Comparatively, in Exodus 32, God is all of those descriptors as the Levites were commanded to show their loyalty to God by slaying their idol-worshiping brothers, neighbors, and friends. While the events are ironic in time and circumstances, what is clear is that God is ruler and judge over all.

Verse 29: Then Moses said, "You have been set apart to the Lord today, for you were against your own sons and brothers, and he has blessed you this day."

Being set apart for God takes commitment, sacrifice, loyalty, and courage, which is accompanied by God's blessings.

Verse 30: The next day Moses said to the people, "You have committed a great sin. But now I will go up to the Lord; perhaps I can make atonement for your sin."

Moses climbed back up the mountain seeking forgiveness. He had both a physical and spiritual burden as the leader of a disloyal, rebellious people.

Verse 31-32: 31 So Moses went back to the Lord and said, "Oh, what a great sin these people have committed! They have made themselves gods of gold. 32 But now, please forgive their sin—but if not, then blot me out of the book you have written."

Moses returned to the mountain and informed God of their sin. (God had already told Moses!) Moses asked for forgiveness or to erase his name. He took responsibility for his people's actions.

Verse 33: The Lord replied to Moses, "Whoever has sinned against me I will blot out of my book.

Verse 34: Now go, lead the people to the place I spoke of, and my angel will go before you. However, when the time comes for me to punish, I will punish them for their sin."

Verse 35: And the Lord struck the people with a plague because of what they did with the calf Aaron had made.

And the Lord struck the people with a plague because of what they did with the calf Aaron had made. If the people were going to act like the Egyptians, then God was going to give them the consequence that he gave to the Egyptians: a plague.

Reflection:

1. Who has influenced me to sin? When have I blamed my sin on the actions of another's influences or pressure?

2. How quickly have I turned from God? Especially when God was not present to me?

3. Do I tire of waiting on God and go to "other gods" for answers (mystics, fortune tellers, horoscopes, therapists)?

4. Can the Lord change his mind? (Vs. 14) What do I want to change God's mind about?

5. What is my gold calf that takes God's place with my treasures, time, and attention?

6. God tells Moses to go in verse 7 and 24. How is God telling me to go? In what way?

7. God holds sinners accountable. How have I accounted for my sins? When have I had to drink the bitter cup of consequences after being disobedient to God?

8. Are there any elements of my church's worship services that have been influenced by the world, the current culture?

9. Was Moses' anger justified in smashing the tablets with God's commandments on them? What was Moses' consequence for this show of anger?

10. Have I had to set myself apart from a family member, friend, or neighbor because of their lack of morals or unGodly lifestyle? How difficult was it to make the distinction in favor of following God?

11. When have I had to intercede for someone who was under my leadership? As a leader, do I take responsibility for the actions of those under my leadership? How?

12. Does God expect individual responsibility for our actions?

Response:

_____

_____

_____

_____

_____

_____

_____

_____

_____

_____

_____

_____

_____

DAY**33**

Exodus
Chapter Thirty-Three

Summary:
God needs purity and cannot be in the presence of sin.

Verse 1: "Go!"

Verse 3: Go up to the land flowing with milk and honey. But I will not go with you, because you are a stiff-necked people and I might destroy you on the way."

God sent his angel to lead them because even God set his limits with how much he could tolerate sin and rebellion without completely destroying the rebellious people.

Verse 4: When the people heard these distressing words, they began to mourn and no one put on any ornaments.

Verse 5-6: 5 For the Lord had said to Moses, "Tell the Israelites, 'You are a stiff-necked people. If I were to go with you even for a moment, I might destroy you. Now take off your ornaments and I will decide what to do with you.'" 6 So the Israelites stripped off their ornaments at Mount Horeb.

God gave some wait time until consequences were assigned. Jewelry for the gold calf, but no jewelry in God's sight.

Verse 8: God still appeared as a cloud in the Tent of Meeting.

Verse 11: The Lord would speak to Moses face to face as one speaks to a friend.

Verse 13: (Moses asked God) "If you are pleased with me, teach me your ways so I may know you and continue to find favor with you. Remember that this nation is your people."

Verse 14: The Lord replied, "My Presence will go with you, and I will give you rest."

Verse 15-16: 15 Then Moses said to him, "If your Presence does not go with us, do not send us up from here. 16 How will anyone know that you are pleased with me and with your people unless you go with us? What else will distinguish me and your people from all the other people on the face of the earth?"

The presence of God sets us apart from all other people on earth.

Verse 17: And the Lord said to Moses, "I will do the very thing you have asked, because I am pleased with you and I know you by name."

Verse 18: Moses: Then Moses said, "Now show me your glory."

Verse 19-20: 19 And the Lord said, "I will cause all my goodness to pass in front of you, and I will proclaim my name, the Lord, in your presence. I will have mercy on whom I will have mercy, and I will have compassion on whom I will have compassion. 20 But," he said, "you cannot see my face, for no one may see me and live."

No face to face exchanges between Moses and God.

Verse 22-23: 23 "When my glory passes by, I will put you in a cleft in the rock and cover you with my hand until I have passed by. 23 Then I will remove my hand and you will see my back; but my face must not be seen."

Reflection:

1. When have I been stubborn or rebellious with God?

2. Do I speak with God as a friend? Face to face?

3. Do I pray, "Let me know your ways..."? How can I understand God more fully?

4. When has God been present with me to give me rest?

5. How do I know that I am set apart? What evidence do I have?

6. When have I seen God's glorious presence?

7. When has God shown me mercy?

8. When has God shown me compassion?

Response:

_____

_____

_____

_____

_____

_____

_____

_____

_____

_____

_____

DAY**34**

Exodus
Chapter Thirty-Four

Summary:

Verse 1: The Lord said to Moses, "Chisel out two stone tablets like the first ones, and I will write on them the words that were on the first tablets, which you broke.

Ouch! God provided the first set. Moses had to chisel the replacement set and take the stone tablets back up the mountain. This was a consequence for having thrown them down and destroyed them in his anger. While Moses chiseled the stone tablets, God was going to inscribe the words himself. Apparently God wanted no one to mis-chisel or misinterpret his commands. Both times God inscribed his Commandments. (Later in 34:27 God had Moses write commands and instructions regarding the firstborn and festivals.)

Verse 2: Be ready in the morning, and then come up on Mount Sinai. Present yourself to me there on top of the mountain.

Verse 3: No one is to come with you or be seen anywhere on the mountain; not even the flocks and herds may graze in front of the mountain."

This was different from the previous ascent to meet God: new terms of agreement.

Verse 5: Then the Lord came down in the cloud and stood there with him and proclaimed his name, the Lord.

"Yahweh!"

Verses 6-7: And he passed in front of Moses, proclaiming, "The Lord, the Lord, the compassionate and gracious God, slow to anger, abounding in love and faithfulness, 7 maintaining love to thousands, and forgiving wickedness, rebellion and sin. Yet he does not leave the guilty unpunished; he punishes the children and their children for the sin of the parents to the third and fourth generation."

God describes himself as having compassion, mercy, slow to anger, unfailing love, faithfulness, "to 1,000 generations", forgiver of iniquity, rebellion, and sin. However, the entire family line is affected through the third and fourth generations.

Verse 8: Moses hit the ground and worshiped God.

Verse 10: Then the Lord said: "I am making a covenant with you. Before all your people I will do wonders never before done in any nation in all the world. The people you live among will see how awesome is the work that I, the Lord, will do for you.

God referred to the Israelites as "all your people" rather than "all my people".

Verse 12: God reframes and restates how to obey his first commandment. No treaties with people in the Promised Land - no other gods - "you will get trapped and follow other gods."

Verse 15: No marriages with foreigners. No molten gods of metal.

Verse 18: Festival of Unleavened Bread

Verse 19: First born belongs to God - You must buy back - redeem. "No one may appear before me without an offering.

Verse 21: Sabbath

Verse 22: Festival of Harvest - men only appear before God 3x annually

Verse 26: Bring the very best of the first harvest.

Verse 27: Write down all these instructions. (Apparently God didn't trust the people's ability to remember, based on past experiences.)

Verse 28: Moses - ate no bread and drank no water for 40 days, and the Lord wrote the ten commandments (terms of the Covenant) on the stone tablets.

Verse 29: Moses face becomes radiant in the presence of God.

Verse 32: Moses delivers the ten commandments.

Verse 33: Moses veils his face and only uncovers his face when speaking to the Lord.

Reflection:

1. Do I prepare myself to be ready each morning to climb to the presence of God?

2. Do I reflect God's qualities of being compassionate, merciful, slow to anger, loving, faithful, and forgiving? How can I grow to be more like God?

3. The choices I make today matter to future generations. How have my choices either blessed or cursed my children and grandchildren? Are there any adjustments that I can make today that can end a curse and begin a blessing? (unhealthy or healthy lifestyle choices, broken or restored relationships, dropping out of church or finding a strong church community, selfishness or servanthood)

4. Have I made treaties with worldly people that caused me to compromise my faithfulness to God and his commands?

5. Do I give God the very best of my "first harvest"?

6. Have I been able to fast for 40 days and nights from food and/or water to become closer to God?

7. How grateful am I that God gave Moses and the Israelites a second chance for a covenant relationship through the commandments on the stone tablets?

8. Why is it important for me to record, journal, write what God has spoken to me and what God has done for me in my life? What would I put in writing so far?

Response:

_____

_____

_____

_____

_____

_____

_____

_____

_____

DAY**35**

Exodus
Chapter Thirty-Five

Summary:

Verse 4-9: 4 Moses said to the whole Israelite community, "This is what the Lord has commanded: 5 From what you have, take an offering for the Lord. Everyone who is willing is to bring to the Lord an offering of gold, silver and bronze; 6 blue, purple and scarlet yarn and fine linen; goat hair; 7 ram skins dyed red and another type of durable leather[a]; acacia wood; 8 olive oil for the light; spices for the anointing oil and for the fragrant incense; 9 and onyx stones and other gems to be mounted on the ephod and breastpiece.

God commanded an offering for his temple, but only from those who were willing.

Verse 10: "All who are skilled among you are to come and make everything the Lord has commanded:

Verse 20-22: 20 Then the whole Israelite community withdrew from Moses' presence, 21 and everyone who was willing and whose heart moved them came and brought an offering to the Lord for the work on the tent of meeting, for all its service, and for the sacred garments. 22 All who were willing, men and women alike, came and brought gold jewelry of all kinds: brooches, earrings, rings and ornaments. They all presented their gold as a wave offering to the Lord.

Verse 29: All the Israelite men and women who were willing brought to the Lord freewill offerings for all the work the Lord through Moses had commanded them to do.

Verse 34: Bezalel and Oholiab were given the ability to teach others their skills - excelled as craftsmen and designers.

Reflection:

1. What are my gifts to use for the Lord?

2. What can I share/teach others in serving the Lord?

3. Have I ever been called up for special assignments for the Lord?

4. Am I "eager to help in the work the Lord has given" me?

5. When has my heart been stirred and my spirit moved to bring a sacred offering to the Lord?

Response:

_____

_____

_____

_____

_____

_____

_____

_____

DAY**36**

Exodus
Chapter Thirty-Six

Summary:

Verse 3-5: 3 They received from Moses all the offerings the Israelites had brought to carry out the work of constructing the sanctuary. And the people continued to bring freewill offerings morning after morning. 4 So all the skilled workers who were doing all the work on the sanctuary left what they were doing 5 and said to Moses, "The people are bringing more than enough for doing the work the Lord commanded to be done."

Verse 8-37 Bezalel followed exactly God's instructions for building the Tabernacle.

Reflection:

1. Do I give "more than enough" to the point where I am asked to stop giving?

2. Do church leaders or missionaries ever say, "We have enough?"

3. Bezalel was a designer and craftsman, but followed God in each detail. He didn't have to put "his stamp" on the design. Am I the same way when asked to design or craft something in the name of the Lord or in the name of the church?

Response:

_____

_____

_____

DAY**37**

Exodus
Chapter Thirty-Seven

Summary:

The making of the Ark, Table, Lampstand, and Altar of Incense.

Verse 1-2: 1 Bezalel made the ark of acacia wood—two and a half cubits long, a cubit and a half wide, and a cubit and a half high. 2 He overlaid it with pure gold, both inside and out, and made a gold molding around it.

Verse 10-12: They made the table of acacia wood—two cubits long, a cubit wide and a cubit and a half high. 11 Then they overlaid it with pure gold and made a gold molding around it. 12 They also made around it a rim a handbreadth [d] wide and put a gold molding on the rim.

Notice that Bezalel is given sole credit for having constructed the ark (the pronoun "he"). For the construction of the table, lampstand, and altar of incense, the pronoun "they" is used.

Reflection:

1. Bezalel was a master craftsman who was given the assignment to build the ark, the Ark of the Covenant, where all the precious items of the Exodus were held as evidence of God's leading the Israelites out of captivity. Is there a skill or a talent that I am using for God as evidence of living out my purpose in life for him? How does God want me to use my talents in his kingdom on earth?

2. All of these items are adorned with pure gold. God doesn't want me to give him myself and my offerings with defects. He wants the best of who I am. Am I giving God a life of purest gold, the best of who I am, as his child?

3. If I were to construct an Ark of the Covenant that held evidence of God working in my life, what items would be contained inside? What would I consider to be sacred to keep and to remember what God has done for me?

Response:

_____

_____

_____

_____

_____

_____

_____

_____

_____

_____

_____

_____

DAY**38**

Exodus
Chapter Thirty-Eight

Summary:

Verse 21:These are the amounts of the materials used for the tabernacle, the tabernacle of the covenant law, which were recorded at Moses' command by the Levites under the direction of Ithamar son of Aaron, the priest.

Inventory of materials used in building the Tabernacle of the Covenant and the amounts of materials were compiled by the Levites. Ithamar, son of Aaron, was the recorder.

Verse 22: Bezabel, son of Uri, grandson of Hur, of the tribe of Judah, made everything just as the Lord commanded Moses.

Verse 26: Silver came from the tax collected from each man (21 years old+)

Everyone contributed! Craftsmen followed God's exact instructions: his "manual". Levites took inventory and showed accountability to God and the people what was collected and used in the construction of God's temple. .

Reflection:

1. When God asked me to do something specifically, how much do I insert my own will or desires or design into the Lord's request?

2. How important was it for Bezalel to follow instructions to the finest detail? Why?

Response:

_____

_____

_____

_____

_____

_____

_____

_____

_____

_____

_____

_____

_____

DAY**39**

Exodus
Chapter Thirty-Nine

Summary:

God's representatives were to be beautifully clothed and set apart with all the world's riches in gems and materials (both God made and man made.)

The priests represented the tribes of Israel with the two onyx stones:

Red carnelian, green peridot, emerald, turquoise, blue lapis lazuli, white moonstone;

Orange jacinth, agate, purple amethyst, blue green beryl, onyx, green jasper.

All set in gold filigree.

(This description reads like the ultimate "mother's ring" of her children!)

The name engraved on each one like a seal!

Bells and pomegranates on the hems of the robes

Sacred medallion of pure gold - the badge of holiness - engraved "Holy to the Lord"

Verse 32-33: 32 So all the work on the tabernacle, the tent of meeting, was completed. The Israelites did everything just as the Lord commanded Moses. 33 Then they brought the tabernacle to Moses...

For anyone who has gone through an inspection or audit by a boss or the government, just imagine how Bezalel, Oholiab, and the other skilled laborers must have felt when all the work was completed and ready for Moses to inspect. For anyone who has been responsible for an inspection or audit, imagine how Moses must have felt when checking to ensure that ALL of God's commands were obeyed from design to completion.

Verse 43: Moses inspected all the work, then blessed them.

Whew! Can you hear a corporate sigh of relief from Bezalel and Oholiab and company?

Reflection:

1. How much does God love his people as shown through his instructions?

2. How holy is God to bind us in covenant through a spectacular Tabernacle and Priests?

3. What gems do I love? Which would I want with my name engraved?

4. What level of responsibility must God have given to his chosen priests and people? Each tribe?

5. What tribe am I from?

Response:

_____

_____

_____

_____

_____

_____

_____

_____

_____

_____

_____

_____

_____

DAY**40**

Exodus
Chapter Forty

Summary:
It is finished!

Difference between the Egypt experience and the Desert Experience:

    a. Pharaoh kept Moses and the people at a distance; God met face to face with Moses and came into a covenant relationship with the Israelites;

    b. People slaved for bricks in Egypt; God served the people manna and quail in the desert;

    c. People treated like animals in Egypt; people's tribal names were engraved on precious gemstones according to God's commands;

    d. Forced labor in Egypt; covenant relationship with God in the desert

Verse 9: God to Moses: "Take the anointing oil and anoint the tabernacle and everything in it; consecrate it and all its furnishings, and it will be holy.

Verse 12: Aaron and sons washed with water, dressed, anointed, and were set apart.

Verse 20: He took the tablets of the covenant law and placed them in the ark, attached the poles to the ark and put the atonement cover over it.

Moses took the stone tablets inscribed with the terms of the covenant and placed them inside the ark.

Verse 22-23: 22 Moses placed the table in the tent of meeting on the north side of the tabernacle outside the curtain 23 and set out the bread on it before the Lord, as the Lord commanded him.

Moses set the table for the Lord with the Passover bread on it.

Verse 25: Then he lit the lamps in the Lord's presence, just as the Lord commanded.

Verse 27: Fragrant incense in place

Verse 28: Curtain in place

Verse 31: Aaron and sons washed hands and feet each time entering the tabernacle

Verse 34-35: 34 Then the cloud covered the tent of meeting, and the glory of the Lord filled the tabernacle. 35 Moses could not enter the tent of meeting because the cloud had settled on it, and the glory of the Lord filled the tabernacle.

This example of God coming to a man-made tabernacle to be with the man, Moses, is such a personal, powerful, climactic display of God's desire to be in relationship with his people. However, God's glory takes up every part of this inhabitable space that there is no room for Moses, for the man of God.

Similarly with Jesus in John 1:14 when the Son of God came to dwell on earth and showed his glory, he made a way for the spirit of God to dwell in us. Through Jesus' death on the cross for all our sins and his resurrection from the dead, now his Holy Spirit can dwell in us, his new tabernacle! Our hearts are his tabernacle today, and if his spirit is to fill us with his presence, then there is only room for God.

John 1:14 The Word became flesh and made his dwelling among us. We have seen his glory, the glory of the one and only Son, who came from the Father, full of grace and truth.

God's presence in our tabernacle of hearts cannot share space with any other idol, person, or possession. Review his first commandment:

Exodus 20:2-3: 2 "I am the Lord your God, who brought you out of Egypt, out of the land of slavery. 3 You shall have no other gods before me."

Verse 36-37: 36 In all the travels of the Israelites, whenever the cloud lifted from above the tabernacle, they would set out; 37 but if the cloud did not lift, they did not set out—until the day it lifted.

Verse 38: So the cloud of the Lord was over the tabernacle by day, and fire was in the cloud by night, in the sight of all the Israelites during all their travels.

This reads like a "happily ever after" story, except that the book ends before the Israelites reach the Promised Land. We want to read the sequel! We know that they finally arrive, but that story is in the book of Joshua. As for the book of Exodus, the people were set free and exited Egypt, the land of their bondage and slavery. Some of them, Moses included, survived the wilderness, although Moses was not permitted by God to enter the Promised Land. Moses, too, suffered consequences for not being obedient to God in all matters.

Consider the difference between what God commanded and what Moses said and did in Numbers 20:7-12:

7 The Lord said to Moses, 8 "Take the staff, and you and your brother Aaron gather the assembly together. Speak to that rock before their eyes and it will pour out its water. You will bring water out of the rock for the community so they and their livestock can drink." 9 So Moses took the staff from the Lord's presence, just as he commanded him. 10 He and Aaron gathered the assembly together in front of the rock and Moses said to them, "Listen, you rebels, must we bring you water out of this rock?" 11 Then Moses raised his arm and struck the rock twice with his staff. Water gushed out, and the community and their livestock drank. 12 But the Lord said to Moses and Aaron, "Because you did not trust in me enough to honor me as holy in the sight of the Israelites, you will not bring this community into the land I give them."

Instead of speaking to the rock, Moses chastised the people and took credit ("we") for bringing water from the rock. God could have chosen to strike Moses dead for disobeying; there is enough evidence in Exodus to consider that as a possibility. Instead, Moses' punishment was his exclusion from living in the Promised Land. Imagine his disappointment; after all he had done right, he had lost the big reward from his sin against God. However, Moses was blessed with a long life of 120 years, surviving the wilderness still with great strength and strong eyes to see the Promised Land from a distance.

Deuteronomy 34:1-7: 1 Then Moses climbed Mount Nebo from the plains of Moab to the top of Pisgah, across from Jericho. There the Lord showed him the whole land—from Gilead to Dan, 2 all of Naphtali, the territory of Ephraim and Manasseh, all the land of Judah as far as the Mediterranean Sea, 3 the Negev and the whole region from the Valley of Jericho, the City of Palms, as far as Zoar. 4 Then the Lord said to him, "This is the land I promised on oath to Abraham, Isaac and Jacob when I said, 'I will give it to your descendants.' I have let you see it with your eyes, but you will not cross over into it." 5 And Moses the servant of the Lord died there in Moab, as the Lord had said. 6 He buried him in Moab, in the valley opposite Beth Peor, but to this day no one knows where his grave is. 7 Moses was a hundred and twenty years old when he died, yet his eyes were not weak nor his strength gone.

It is significant that the verse says that God buried Moses in a valley in Moab in an unmarked grave. Consider the irony of the death of Moses, a former Prince of Egypt, who would normally have risen to be king and deserving of a grave as magnificent as an Egyptian pyramid. As leader of Israel, because of his disobedience to God, Moses cannot be honored at his gravesite, nor is there a mountain to serve as a memorial to this patriarch, just somewhere in "the valley opposite Beth Peor". The honor given to Moses today comes through oral and written tradition passed down by his future generations. To tell the story of Moses is to tell the first commandment of the sovereignty of God, who commands complete obedience and loyalty in his desire for a relationship with his people.

Like Moses, Aaron did not get to see the Promised Land because of his disobedience to God at the waters of Meribah. Aaron died in the wilderness at the age of 123. However, God blessed Aaron by telling him in advance that he was going to die and that he, his son, and Moses would go up Mount Hor, where the son would step into his father's leadership role. Symbolically and physically, Aaron's garments were removed and put on his son, Eleazar. Then Aaron was "gathered to his people", an ancient expression for joining his ancestors in death.

Numbers 20:23-26: 23 At Mount Hor, near the border of Edom, the Lord said to Moses and Aaron, 24 "Aaron will be gathered to his people. He will not enter the land I give the Israelites, because both of you rebelled against my command at the waters of Meribah. 25 Get Aaron and his son Eleazar and take them up Mount Hor. 26 Remove Aaron's garments and put them on his son Eleazar, for Aaron will be gathered to his people; he will die there.

For disobedience to God, a desert death came to all males old enough to go into battle when leaving Egypt.

Joshua 5:6 The Israelites had moved about in the wilderness forty years until all the men who were of military age when they left Egypt had died, since they had not obeyed the Lord. For the Lord had sworn to them that they would not see the land he had solemnly promised their ancestors to give us, a land flowing with milk and honey.

By this time, Moses had to have wondered what would happen to him after seeing Aaron die for the Meribah mishap and after seeing all of the older men dead in the desert. Moses would learn that he, too, would be "gathered to his people" after he saw the Promised Land.

Numbers 27:12-14: 12 Then the Lord said to Moses, "Go up this mountain in the Abarim Range and see the land I have given the Israelites. 13 After you have seen it, you too will be gathered to your people, as your brother Aaron was,14 for when the community rebelled at the waters in the Desert of Zin, both of you disobeyed my command to honor me as holy before their eyes."

Moses' torch of leadership was not passed to his son, but to the son of Nun and Moses' aide since his youth. Joshua was described by God as having the spirit of wisdom in him. Moses was to bring Joshua before the whole assembly of the people, to lay hands on him, and to commission him with "some" of Moses' authority so that the people would obey him.

Numbers 27:16-23: Moses said to the Lord, 16 "May the Lord, the God who gives breath to all living things, appoint someone over this community 17 to go out and come in before them, one who will lead them out and bring them in, so the Lord's people will not be like sheep without a shepherd." 18 So the Lord said to Moses, "Take Joshua son of Nun, a man in whom is the spirit of leadership, and lay your hand on him. 19 Have him stand before Eleazar the priest and the entire assembly and commission him in their presence. 20 Give him some of your authority so the whole Israelite community will obey him. 21 He is to stand before Eleazar the priest, who will obtain decisions for him by inquiring of the Urim before the Lord. At his command he and the entire community of the Israelites will go out, and at his command they will come in." 22 Moses did as the Lord commanded him. He took Joshua and had him stand before Eleazar the priest and the whole assembly. 23 Then he laid his hands on him and commissioned him, as the Lord instructed through Moses.

Note the difference in leadership from Moses and Aaron to Joshua and Eleazar. Both younger men had walked side by side with two great men of God, and they witnessed the outcomes of their predecessors' obedience and disobedience. The young men's signs of God's authority were significantly different from the staff of Moses or Aaron: the staff that signaled so many miracles as the Israelites were "shepherded" out of slavery and to the Promised Land of freedom. Different from their predecessors, Eleazar used the Urim to help Joshua with decisions, and Joshua used his sword by which he fought the Amalekites and won (Joshua 17:13), and his flint knives which he made himself for the purpose of circumcising the young men of age who had survived the wilderness, as God had commanded him.

However, when the time came for the miracle of crossing the Jordan River, Joshua did not use swords or knives, but his words that were backed by the authority of God. Unlike Moses and Aaron, in complete obedience, Joshua spoke God's commands to the people. Note the difference between Moses and Aaron at Meribah and Joshua at the Jordan River. Moses and Aaron deviated from God's command for them to take their staff, come before the people, speak to the rock to make water flow for the people complaining of thirst and quarreling with them. Instead, Moses chose to speak derision to the people and beat the rock with a staff twice, whether out of anger or distrust in God or both can be debated. (Public speaking had never been Moses' strength, as he himself attested, but God had asked Moses to speak to the rock, not to people. Moses had one task to do: talk to the rock. He blew it by overstepping God.)

In contrast, Joshua obeyed the words of the Lord exactly and spoke to the people, telling them to "come and listen to the words of the Lord." He told them that the ark of the covenant would go ahead of them into the overflowing waters of the Jordan River, that twelve men would carry the ark and set foot in the Jordan, where the waters would then be cut off so that they could cross over to the Promised Land. As God's leader charged with completing the task of getting the people to the Promised Land, Joshua showed complete obedience. In addition, God commanded the people to demonstrate their obedience before the miracle happened.

Joshua 3:9-13: 9 Joshua said to the Israelites, "Come here and listen to the words of the Lord your God. 10 This is how you will know that the living God is among you and that he will certainly drive out before you the Canaanites, Hittites, Hivites, Perizzites, Girgashites, Amorites and Jebusites. 11 See, the ark of the covenant of the Lord of all the earth will go into the Jordan ahead of you. 12 Now then, choose twelve men from the tribes of Israel, one from each tribe. 13 And as soon as the priests who carry the ark of the Lord—the Lord of all the earth—set foot in the Jordan, its waters flowing downstream will be cut off and stand up in a heap."

This new pattern of leadership and obedience continued to the battle for the city of Jericho, where God gave instructions to Joshua for the people to march for six days before seeing the miraculous victory over Jericho on the seventh day. (Joshua 6)

We must be mindful of these lessons, particularly for leaders in our families and communities. We must always remember that God leads the leaders in all circumstances, and that God alone is to receive the honor and glory. Complete obedience to God leads to many blessings and successes. Disobedience to God results in undesirable consequences of varying degrees.

As disheartening for us to imagine Moses looking at the Promised Land and knowing that he will never live there, let us also imagine the joy Moses may have felt knowing that his leadership was instrumental in bringing his families out of bondage and to their "home" of God's promises. Unlike Aaron or the other men who died in the wilderness, God allowed Moses to live to see the fruit of his labor, even though he didn't taste it himself. That must have given Moses some sense of joy and contentment as he climbed yet another mountain, Mount Nebo, where God showed Moses the fulfillment of the Promised Land. The descendants of Moses would prosper under the new leadership of Joshua, and God would always be with them.

8 The Israelites grieved for Moses in the plains of Moab thirty days, until the time of weeping and mourning was over. 9 Now Joshua son of Nun was filled with the spirit of wisdom because Moses had laid his hands on him. So the Israelites listened to him and did what the Lord had commanded Moses. 10 Since then, no prophet has risen in Israel like Moses, whom the Lord knew face to face, 11 who did all those signs and wonders the Lord sent him to do in Egypt—to Pharaoh and to all his officials and to his whole land. 12 For no one has ever shown the mighty power or performed the awesome deeds that Moses did in the sight of all Israel.

Reflection:

1. How is my journey with God? Do I see God guiding me by day and night? How?

2. How different was life under Pharaoh and life under God and Moses? How different is my life after asking Jesus to be my Lord and Savior of my life?

3. Aaron and sons were washed, dressed, anointed, and set apart. How does this compare to me being set apart for God? How am I washed? Dressed? Anointed? Set apart?

4. When I am ready for my Promised Land, will God find me worthy to enter and taste the full goodness of his promises?

5. Am I certain that my family will enter the Promised Land? If not, what must I do to help them in their journey?

6. To whom might God transfer my leadership role in my family or community? How might I help to prepare them for the time when I am "gathered to my people" in death?

7. What's next? What book of the bible do I want to read and study more in depth?

Response:

_____

_____

_____

_____

_____

_____

_____

_____

_____

_____

Conclusion

Conclusion

We began this forty-day devotional by imagining ourselves as descendants of one of the families or tribes of Israel. We imagined hearing from our forefathers how some of our families survived and some died during the great Exodus from Egypt; how the Great Grandfather Moses led us through all the trials and victories; and how God stayed faithful night and day. Imagine how Moses may have felt as the families' leader: perhaps exhausted from trips up and down the mountain; perhaps embarrassed to constantly ask God to forgive his ungrateful, disobedient people; perhaps exhilarated from his face-to-face encounters with God; no doubt elated to see the parting of the Red Sea; and certainly victorious when all his enemies were destroyed by God's design. Imagine how Moses must have felt when he was only permitted to view, but not enter, the Promised Land from the nearby Mount Nebo. Moses had not trusted God enough to do exactly what he was commanded to do. His disobedience was costly. How he must have regretted his actions.

Let's circle back to the introduction of this devotional that began with these words:

> *"Have you ever been disappointed in yourself? In other people? So has God...all the time. He appoints us to be his people; in return, we disappoint him on a regular basis, yet he forgives and loves us. He wants more for us, so he always gives us another chance to keep our appointment. Don't believe it? Read Exodus. Our God never gives up on us. Never."*

After just forty days of reading and reflecting on Exodus, we can apply lessons learned to our own lives. We can retell the Exodus story to the next generations with our own testimonies of God's faithfulness (and perhaps our times of struggling to obey God's commands). We can provide them with a bible for them to read and study the Word of God, where there is more to learn from the books of Numbers, Deuteronomy, Joshua, and beyond to our salvation story of Jesus' birth, death, and resurrection, and his coming again as promised in the book of Revelation! This is our ancestors' legacy for us to pass on to our children; this is our God, our One who saves, our God who forgives, and our God who restores. Our God never gives up on us. Never. To God be all the honor and glory for his mercy, grace, and provision.

Deuteronomy 10:12-15: 12 And now, Israel, what does the Lord your God ask of you but to fear the Lord your God, to walk in obedience to him, to love him, to serve the Lord your God with all your heart and with all your soul, 13 and to observe the Lord's commands and decrees that I am giving you today for your own good? 14 To the Lord your God belong the heavens, even the highest heavens, the earth and everything in it. 15 Yet the Lord set his affection on your ancestors and loved them, and he chose you, their descendants, above all the nations—as it is today.

Notes for Further Study of Exodus from Mentors and Friends

Notes for Further Study of Exodus from Mentors and Friends

The book of Exodus is the history of an imperfect leader of an imperfect people, who were called by a perfect God to be his people. That is their legacy for all generations. That is our legacy, if we call ourselves God's children and follow his commands: to love him and to love others. Pastor Felix R. Escobar, my mentor and friend from Argentina, shared his notes from a 1984 Bible study with Pastor Arturo Schultz on the book of Exodus. Below is a transcription from Spanish to English for further insights.

The Three Stages of Moses' Life

1. 40 years in Egypt - Intellectual preparation

As the adopted son of the daughter of Pharaoh, Moses had the possibility of occupying the proudest throne on earth at that time, but he chose to be obedient to God, to the teaching of his mother and her religion.

Acts 7:22 Moses was educated in all the wisdom of the Egyptians and was powerful in speech and action.

Moses had the intention of freeing his people or the people of God from slavery when he intervened in the revenge of a compatriot of his and killed the Egyptian. This first attempt failed. The people were not prepared to receive him as leader, so he fled.

2. 40 years in the desert - Spiritual Preparation

Being exposed to solitude and deprived of the luxurious palace, Moses lived in the desert, where God in his great love and wisdom was able to prepare his servant.

There Moses had time to meditate, both on the suffering of

his people and on the promises of God, and he familiarized himself with the region through which he would later take the people of Israel. There Moses married Zipporah; his father-in-law was Jethro, a Midianite priest; and Moses and Zipporah had two sons, Gershom and Eliezer.

3. 40 years leading the people of Israel - His work

Moses had already learned not to trust in his own strength, but in the power of God. Filled with that power, he went to Egypt and there God manifested himself through wonders and healings, freeing the people from slavery.

The book of Genesis tells of the creation and fall of man, and the book of Exodus brings us the message of redemption from slavery through the powerful arm of God. It begins with a great necessity for God and ends with the glory of God upon the tabernacle.

The Three Parts of Exodus

1. The Call - Chapters 1-12:36

2. The Redemption - Chapters 12:37-18:27

3. The Covenant - Chapters 19-40

The Passover Lamb Parallels Jesus, the Lamb of God

The Paschal Lamb in Exodus 12 points to Christ as the Lamb of God in John 1:29.

The lamb had to be without defect in Exodus 12:5.

The animals you choose must be year-old males without defect, and you may take them from the sheep or the goats.

Compare the Paschal lamb to Jesus as the Lamb of God in 1 Peter 1:18-19.

For you know that it was not with perishable things such as silver or gold that you were redeemed from the empty way of life handed down to you from your ancestors, 19 but with the precious blood of Christ, a lamb without blemish or defect.

The Paschal lamb's blood was spread and applied in Exodus 12:7

Then they are to take some of the blood and put it on the sides and tops of the doorframes of the houses where they eat the lambs.

Compare the lamb's blood to the bloodshed of Jesus Christ in Hebrews 9:14.

How much more, then, will the blood of Christ, who through the eternal Spirit offered himself unblemished to God, cleanse our consciences from acts that lead to death, so that we may serve the living God!

The bones of the lamb were not to be broken in Exodus 12:46.

"It must be eaten inside the house; take none of the meat outside the house. Do not break any of the bones.

Compare this to Jesus, the Lamb of God, on the cross in John 19:33-37

33 But when they came to Jesus and found that he was already dead, they did not break his legs. 34 Instead, one of the soldiers pierced Jesus' side with a spear, bringing a sudden flow of blood and water. 35 The man who saw it has given testimony, and his testimony is true. He knows that he tells the truth, and he testifies so that you also may believe. 36 These things happened so that the scripture would be fulfilled: "Not one of his bones will be broken," 37 and, as another scripture says, "They will look on the one they have pierced."

The Passover was the only way of salvation for the people of Israel. Jesus as the Lamb of God, is the only way of salvation for us.

The Tabernacle Parallels in the New Testament

Tabernacle's design of redemption - *Hebrews verses 8:5-6: 5 They serve at a sanctuary that is a copy and shadow of what is in heaven. This is why Moses was warned when he was about to build the tabernacle: "See to it that you make everything according to the pattern shown to you on the mountain." 6 But in fact the ministry Jesus has received is as superior to theirs as the covenant of which he is mediator is superior to the old one, since the new covenant is established on better promises.*

Tabernacle's altar of sacrifice - *Hebrews 9:22 In fact, the law requires that nearly everything be cleansed with blood, and without the shedding of blood there is no forgiveness.*

Tabernacle's table of the breads - *John 6:35 Then Jesus declared, "I am the bread of life. Whoever comes to me will never go hungry, and whoever believes in me will never be thirsty.*

Tabernacle's lampstand of gold - *John 8:12 When Jesus spoke again to the people, he said, "I am the light of the world. Whoever follows me will never walk in darkness, but will have the light of life.*

Tabernacle's incense, the sign of the presence of God - *Hebrews 7:25 Therefore he is able to completely save those who come to God through him, because he always lives to intercede for them.*

Tabernacle's atonement - *Matthew 28:20 and teaching them to obey everything I have commanded you. And surely I am with you always, to the very end of the age."*

The Nature and Revelation of God in Exodus

God is revealed...
> **as Savior** - Exodus 12

> *12:13 The blood will be a sign for you on the houses where you are, and when I see the blood, I will pass over you. No*

destructive plague will touch you when I strike Egypt.

as Guide - Exodus 13

13:21 21 By day the Lord went ahead of them in a pillar of cloud to guide them on their way and by night in a pillar of fire to give them light, so that they could travel by day or night.

as Liberator - Exodus 14

14:30 That day the Lord saved Israel from the hands of the Egyptians, and Israel saw the Egyptians lying dead on the shore.

as Physician - Exodus 15

15:26 He said, "If you listen carefully to the Lord your God and do what is right in his eyes, if you pay attention to his commands and keep all his decrees, I will not bring on you any of the diseases I brought on the Egyptians, for I am the Lord, who heals you."

as Giver of Life - Exodus 16

16:8a Moses also said, "You will know that it was the Lord when he gives you meat to eat in the evening and all the bread you want in the morning,

as Victorious - Exodus 17 - Zechariah 4:6

Exodus 17:14 Then the Lord said to Moses, "Write this on a scroll as something to be remembered and make sure that Joshua hears it, because I will completely blot out the name of Amalek from under heaven."

Zechariah 4:6 So he said to me, "This is the word of the Lord to Zerubbabel: 'Not by might nor by power, but by my Spirit,' says the Lord Almighty.

Debbie Day's "Ten Steps to Healthy Living"

Debbie Day, my friend and colleague, is a children's pastor and evangelist. Debbie is always looking for ways to reach people who don't believe in God or who once believed and have rejected church or the Bible for some reason. In the same format as a lifestyle guru would publish "Ten Habits of Success" or "Ten Ways to Live Longer", Debbie has written an easy-to-understand version of God's Ten Commandments based on those in the book of Exodus: great words for living a daily Godly life.

1. Give credit to Whom it is due (to God)..

2. Don't fall for phony substitutes.

3. Don't misrepresent or misuse the name or character of God.

4. Take time to rest.

5. Show honor to those who parent you.

6. Respect all lives.

7. Honor marriage.

8. Respect what belongs to others.

9. Make your words and actions be true.

10. Be content with what you have.

Jesus said (about the 10 Commandments) as recorded in Mark chapter 12:

"The most important one says, 'People of Israel, you have only one Lord and God .vs 29 You must love him with all your heart, soul, mind, and strength.' vs. 30 The second most important commandment says: ' Love others as much as you love yourself.' No other commandment is more important than these." vs31

Afterword

Afterword

Breath in the Darkness
By Chad Shepherd

Think of the nation of Israel bound in slavery under the might of the Egyptian Pharaoh. Their ancestors had been led there through the promise of Abraham and the salvation from famine through Joseph. Their rejoicing had turned into a hopeless darkness.

Beatings. Forced labor. Nights of weeping. No relief. No escape. No end.

And then things began to happen even within that darkness.

Plagues at night. Wailing from the palaces of Egyptian royalty. Water turning to blood, pestilence and disease and chaos. Blood dripping down their doorways, commanded by the breath of God.

Nightmarish and realized fears in darkness as the Angel of Death shrieked over them in the night sky. They could hear death falling on house after house of their captors, yet this dark night was the beginning of their salvation as they waited with bated breath for God to save them.

Deliverance working in darkness. Cloud by day. Fire by night.

Breath. Wait. There is something about breath. The breath of God. Yes, it was the breath of God that voiced creation. It was the breath of God that first breathed life into Adam and Eve. It was the breath of God that spoke miracles, cried in Gethsemane, gave forgiveness from a cross, screamed out that he felt abandoned on that same cross, and then gasped out, "It is finished."

All in darkness.

It is the same for us now. Jesus working in the darkest of nights.

Just as he took the very keys of death from hell while in the darkness. Just as the temple curtain was torn when Jesus died in the darkness on that blood covered cross. Direct access to God given to us in that moment, in the darkness. Sin defeated in darkness. Atonement made in darkness.

If you find yourself in a dark space now, do not despair, for surely you are in the presence of God. He is not afraid of the darkness. He is there within it. He always has been. He always will be. The darkness cannot overcome him.

That same breath of God called Jesus out of the grave three days later. It was in the darkness that God called Jesus back to life. There is more in your darkness than the hot breath of your enemy. There is the life-giving breath of God.

In the darkness, he was there first. It was from the darkness that he spoke even light itself into being.

In the darkness, he has done his best work. In the light, he proves it.

Breathe deeply his life-giving breath. Take a moment. What can you hear? His voice is calling you, guiding you. What can you see? Let your eyes adjust to see what he wants you to see. Begin to see his light within the darkness.

You need not fear what might be in the darkness when you are with God, who is absolutely in the darkness of night, as well as the light of day. If you find yourself in a space of darkness, take heart and continue believing in the God Who Saves. Trust in the Lord. You are in his holy space of darkness. His best work has already begun and will eventually come to light.

Psalm 68: 20-21: Praise be to the Lord, to God our Savior,
who daily bears our burdens. Our God is a God who saves;
from the Sovereign Lord comes escape from death.

Genesis 1:2:Now the earth was formless and empty, darkness was over the surface of the deep, and the Spirit of God was hovering over the waters.

Genesis 10:21-23: 21 Then the Lord said to Moses, "Stretch out your hand toward the sky so that darkness spreads over Egypt—darkness that can be felt." 22 So Moses stretched out his hand toward the sky, and total darkness covered all Egypt for three days. 23 No one could see anyone else or move about for three days. Yet all the Israelites had light in the places where they lived.

Genesis 15:17-21: 17 When the sun had set and darkness had fallen, a smoking firepot with a blazing torch appeared and passed between the pieces. 18 On that day the Lord made a covenant with Abram and said, "To your descendants I give this land, from the Wadi of Egypt to the great river, the Euphrates— 19 the land of the Kenites, Kenizzites, Kadmonites, 20 Hittites, Perizzites, Rephaites, 21 Amorites, Canaanites, Girgashites and Jebusites."

Deuteronomy 4:10-12: 10 Remember the day you stood before the Lord your God at Horeb, when he said to me, "Assemble the people before me to hear my words so that they may learn to revere me as long as they live in the land and may teach them to their children." 11 You came near and stood at the foot of the mountain while it blazed with fire to the very heavens, with black clouds and deep darkness. 12 Then the Lord spoke to you out of the fire. You heard the sound of words but saw no form; there was only a voice.

Deuteronomy 5:22-24: 22 These are the commandments the Lord proclaimed in a loud voice to your whole assembly there on the mountain from out of the fire, the cloud and the deep darkness; and he added nothing more. Then he wrote them on two stone tablets and gave them to me.

23 When you heard the voice out of the darkness, while the mountain was ablaze with fire, all the leaders of your tribes and your elders came to me. 24 And you said, "The Lord our God has shown us his glory and his majesty, and we have heard his voice from the fire. Today we have seen that a person can live even if God speaks with them.

Joshua 24:7 But they cried to the Lord for help, and he put darkness between you and the Egyptians; he brought the sea over them and covered them. You saw with your own eyes what I did to the Egyptians. Then you lived in the wilderness for a long time.

2 Samuel 2:10-14: 10 He parted the heavens and came down; dark clouds were under his feet. 11 He mounted the cherubim and flew; he soared on the wings of the wind. 12 He made darkness his canopy around him— the dark rain clouds of the sky. 13 Out of the brightness of his presence bolts of lightning blazed forth. 14 The Lord thundered from heaven; the voice of the Most High resounded.

Isaiah 29:15: Woe to those who go to great depths to hide their plans from the Lord, who do their work in darkness and think, "Who sees us? Who will know?"

Isaiah 47:7-8: 7 I form the light and create darkness, I bring prosperity and create disaster; I, the Lord, do all these things. 8 "You heavens above, rain down my righteousness; let the clouds shower it down. Let the earth open wide, let salvation spring up, let righteousness flourish with it; I, the Lord, have created it.

Daniel 2:22 He reveals deep and hidden things; he knows what lies in darkness, and light dwells with him.

Psalm 97:1-3: 1 The Lord reigns, let the earth be glad; let the distant shores rejoice. 2 Clouds and thick darkness surround him; righteousness and justice are the foundation of his throne. 3 Fire goes before him and consumes his foes on every side.

Psalm 139:10-12: 10 even there your hand will guide me, your right hand will hold me fast. 11 If I say, "Surely the darkness will hide me and the light will become night around me," 12 even the darkness will not be dark to you; the night will shine like the day, for darkness is as light to you.

Matthew 4:16: the people living in darkness have seen a great light; on those living in the land of the shadow of death a light has dawned."

Luke 23:44: It was now about noon, and darkness came over the whole land until three in the afternoon, 45 for the sun stopped shining. And the curtain of the temple was torn in two.

Acts 2:20: The sun will be turned to darkness and the moon to blood before the coming of the great and glorious day of the Lord.

1 Peter 2:9: But you are a chosen people, a royal priesthood, a holy nation, God's special possession, that you may declare the praises of him who called you out of darkness into his wonderful light.

Appendix

Appendix

By Nancy Hulshult

This book, *The Manna God: 40 Days in Exodus*, is a sequel to the devotional book based upon Genesis, entitled *Imagine You! 40 Days of Devotions: Finding Your Identity in God's Image*. Francesca King and I collaborated on *Imagine You!*, which became the theme for a weekend retreat for the women of Dayspring Church of God in 2022. This notion of taking 40 days to delve into one book of the Bible has impacted me to love and meditate on God's Word like never before. I thought it might be helpful to share how God guided me through the retreat process based upon prayer and God's Word. The results of prayer and preparation were astounding, as the Holy Spirit was present and powerful from beginning to end.

Table Talk: 40 Days of Prayer

My morning bible study and prayer time take place at my dining room table, where I leave my bible, my journal, my phone, and a Christian book or two. Unlike Moses, we don't have to climb a mountain to meet God. Jesus' death and resurrection paved the way for the Holy Spirit to come into our hearts, where we can commune with God all the time and wherever we are. It was in my prayer space where I began 40 days of prayer for the women who would be coming to the Dayspring Women's Retreat in October of 2022. I had tried previous extended days of fasting and prayer, but this time I was personally invested in praying specifically for the women who invested their time and money in order to seek God in community. Some women were friends, and some women I had not met yet. Each story is a testimony of God hearing our prayers and honoring those who desire to have a closer relationship with him. Here is my 40-day journey of a table talk with God.

The Prep, the Prayer, and the Praise

Preparing for our women's retreat about how women see ourselves in the image of God, I prayed about the general tenets of each of the four sessions: 1. We are created in God's image. 2. Jesus, our Redeemer, gives us the perfect model for living a Godly life. 3. The Holy Spirit connects us all together in the most amazing ways. 4. We have a responsibility to be witnesses for Christ, to share our stories.

Then the Lord gave me the ideas for tangible representations to help us remember each tenet: 1. A colorful scarf for each woman, each scarf with a different design from the silk collection of my cousin, Rebecca. 2. A rock from the creek at Grateful Heart Ministry for each woman to remember Jesus as our Rock of Salvation and ourselves as the Living Stones for his church. I had written the word "Imagine" on each rock and suggested that they may want to use the rock as a representation of their burdens and to throw them away during their prayer walk that afternoon. 3. A dot-to-dot sheet with Christian images of 500-1,000 dots to represent how we connect with the Holy Spirit and the Word of God, starting with step one and finding our way each day until we can see the "big picture" of what God wants for us.

The planning came as easily as lesson planning from my career as an educator, but the prayer part took on a new dimension. Several months before the retreat, I began praying every morning and evening for the group of fifty women who had made their reservations to attend. I found myself resorting to a grocery list style of prayer that included my family, friends, and "the women coming to the retreat." Then I realized that if I didn't know all of their names, how could I possibly connect on a personal and spiritual level with them? I contacted our women's director, Cindy Speakman, for a list of attendees and started to read all 50 names each morning. That also sounded robotic, not just to me, but I'm sure to God as well.

I decided to pray on a deeper level for individuals, so I took the list of 50 names and cut them into 50 strips of paper to put into a plastic bag. After I greeted God and gave thanks for the blessings of a new day, I read through Scripture and took notes that related specifically to the theme of the retreat. I had begun in Genesis and kept moving through the Bible, hoping to read it cover to cover before the retreat, should God have specific messages in mind for us. One day as I highlighted a particular verse, I pulled a slip of paper with a woman's name out of the bag and promised God to pray for that woman and to meditate on that scripture all day. I wrote the verse on the back of the slip of paper with the day's date. I wasn't sure if I could continue this process, but each following day resulted in a highlighted scripture (without forcing it) and a name attached. This became very personal for me.

Over the series of weeks, I felt some incredible sadness, oppression, or burdens for some of the women without knowing their circumstances or any specific causes. I felt so strongly about the need for prayer that I asked the retreat committee to join me in praying over the list. They designated some days of intentional prayer and agreed to add a circle of chairs at the retreat for women to come and ask for specific healing prayer before or after each session. I commissioned a couple of prayer warrior friends to join me for this.

After the last name was assigned a scripture, I sought the Holy Spirit for wisdom about sharing the verses with the women. Should I tell them that I prayed for each of them weeks before the retreat? Should I share which scripture was assigned to them on their day? My answer came on the day that I pulled the name of a young woman who had just gotten baptized and married this past year. The scripture was already highlighted, but I felt that there were some complex concepts that may be difficult for her to understand, such as the word "sanctified." I was tempted to put her name back in the bag and pull another name, but then that would compromise the faith that I had developed in this process. I prayed that other women at her table would help her, especially her mother-in-law. I was shocked the next day when I highlighted a verse within the same chapter and pulled the name of her mother-in-law. I got goosebumps on my arms and thanked God for the confirmation of this process. I couldn't wait to see how God would speak to them through his Word.

During prayer one morning, I received the idea of printing each verse for each woman on paper, dating it, rolling it into a parchment scroll, sealing it with our "Imagine" stickers, and printing their names on the outside. The scrolls had dried leaves and flowers within its parchment, and they looked beautiful. I knew that God was going to "gift" each person with a special Word on that day. I had placed my name into the bag as well. On the day that I pulled my name, it was connected to Matthew 13:10-12 (NIV):

His disciples came and asked him, "Why do you use parables when you talk to the people?" He replied, "You are permitted to understand the secrets of the Kingdom of Heaven, but others are not. To those who listen to my teaching, more understanding will be given, and they will have an abundance of knowledge.

When I meditated on this verse, I realized that the scarves, the scrolls, and a suitcase were forms of teaching through parables. Each tangible item would help the listeners to remember the lesson, or so I had hoped. When I questioned myself about being too dramatic with this approach, I remembered Jesus' use of parables. In this way, God gave me confidence to keep going forward with confidence and with my focus on prayer and the message for the women. I felt that God was assuring me that those women who listened to the message could find more understanding and knowledge for their lives. I had no idea that each woman would receive a supernatural understanding that could only come from God.

When the time came to distribute the scrolls, I had suggested that each woman read her own scroll to herself and share with the others at her table. She could either talk about what the verse(s) meant to her or ask the other women to help her understand the truth in it for her from their perspectives.

As the women began to share, there was weeping at every table. It was the quiet type of tears that started from the heart, way deep down inside, and leaked from their eyes as they spoke. God had a very special Word for each one that was understood. Since I had not known many of the women personally before the retreat, it was surprising to see just how specifically the verse related to each woman's circumstances. The most amazing was the dates recorded. One woman reported that her verse was the same verse that she had spoken over her grandchildren several times between the date that I recorded it and the date of the retreat. God had seen her and her circumstances before, during, and after her struggles with grief. Another woman said that she had just lost her husband, and her verse was "blessed are those that mourn". There was no way that I would have known that to manipulate this process. No one was more amazed than I. This process has taken me to a deeper level and consistency of prayer, combined with the reading of Scripture daily, combined with praising and thanking God for the Holy Spirit that knows how to connect us when we have faith in God. Nothing is impossible with God, and during this retreat, I was even more convinced that God created us, Jesus died for us, the Holy Spirit guides us, and God sees us and everything that we are experiencing in life. To God be the glory!

Session One: The Scarf

Every Thanksgiving as we raised our three sons, our family would travel to Ann Arbor, Michigan with my parents to share the most delicious dinner with Aunt Vera and Uncle Gordy Levenson, Cousin Rebecca, and sometimes cousins Burt, Mark, and Tim when they were home for the holiday. The Michigan male cousins were adventurous, working on fishing boats in Alaskan waters, environmental farming on a kibbutz in Israel, or government work in Thailand. Their careers were fascinating, but not any more fascinating than the craftsmanship of the only female Levenson cousin, Rebecca.

Rebecca remained in the Ann Arbor area working a room sized loom or sewing on a commercial sewing machine to create original designs from bolts of linens and silks, accented with hand carved wooden and bone buttons sent to her by her brothers. Rebecca hand painted silk material with her trademark designs using gingko leaves dipped in gold paint and pressed onto the silk, or she would paint flowers on silk with gel pens and fill in the centers with special inks. She also made her own stationery using parchment paper embedded with dried flowers and leaves. She made her own soaps with infused lavender and sold them in handmade pockets of parchment and yarn. Everything Rebecca made came from her wonderfully inventive brain and her love of nature.

After a feast of turkey, farm made stuffing, homemade cranberry walnut salad, and Aunt Vera's hickory nut pie, we would take a hike down the gravel roads and enjoy the snow covered trees and occasional deer and birds spotted in the surrounding woods. In late afternoon, as the men napped or watched football, often trash talking the Michigan vs. Ohio State rivals, the women would go to Rebecca's house to see her latest fashion designs. I would try on her jackets or scarves and purchase a few at a "first cousin discount" to wear to church or to school. Each was one of a kind, as was Rebecca. She had a bohemian look with her long, thick dark hair, flowing cotton skirts, drawstring blouses, a beautiful smile, and a quiet lilting voice that fit her artsy style.

Just before the COVID-19 pandemic ravaged the country, Rebecca's doctors discovered that she had developed terminal brain cancer with a tumor growing at a fast pace. Rebecca and her husband Karl sought solutions from various cancer treatment centers, but she ended up in a facility to care for her debilitating condition. With COVID in full swing, Rebecca's body contorted into a fetal position as she lost her sight, her smile, the use of her hands, and fell into deep depression with no hope for recovery. Rebecca lay in a bed for more than two years in an unresponsive state. When I would call the long term care facility, I could only speak with the front desk to a nurse, who promised to deliver a message that we loved her, that Jesus loved her, and that we were praying for her. Her husband Karl was devastated and had been in a grieving state for months as Rebecca wasted away. Karl was undergoing several operations and hospital stays himself. I had lost track of him until I saw him active on Facebook and asked him how Rebecca was doing. She had died the previous year. I was shocked.

Karl said that all of Rebecca's things were still in the closets of their condo, and he didn't know what to do with them. He didn't have the strength to pack them up, and he didn't want them hanging on the racks at the local Goodwill. He asked me if I wanted them, and immediately, I offered to drive to Michigan to bring her beautiful designs back with me for safe keeping. I promised to honor Rebecca's memory, either by selling the clothes and giving the money to charity, or by doing something spiritually with them. I had no idea exactly what, but I knew that I would find a good home for each jacket and scarf that was designed by Rebecca. My husband Darrell and I drove to Michigan, visited with Karl, and loaded Rebecca's designs into a 20-foot U-Haul truck. We brought all her finished designs, as well as bolts of materials, including beautiful bolts of colorful silk wrapped in plastic.

As I hung up each scarf and jacket, I ran my hands over the silks embossed with the gingko leaves, her trademark. Ironically, the ginkgo is known as a symbol of longevity, since the ginkgo tree can live for a thousand years with profound endurance. Wikipedia reports that four ginkgos survived the blast at Hiroshima and are still growing today. What could I do to preserve the memory and designs of beautiful Rebecca? I knew the answer would come eventually.

The first connection with Rebecca's scarves came from a group of female evangelists visiting my hometown of Hamilton, Ohio for a revival in an inner city church. We hosted them for a few days and offered a few of Rebecca's scarves as gifts to them. I loved the idea of her scarves around the necks of such spiritual people. The women continue to use the scarves today as mantles to pray over pastors and leaders, and their microphone stands are decorated with a couple of the scarves as they speak the hope of Jesus and encouragement to many people. Rebecca would love this use of her handiwork.

Most recently, at a women's retreat, I packed 50 scarves made by Rebecca into her gift boxes and presented them to the women in a talk about being created in the image of God. Each of us is created in the image of God with our individual God-given talents, skills, personalities, and potential to reflect God in our daily lives. We delight in what has been given to us, not envying others gifts or talents, but putting to use what we have to reflect the glory of God in us. As each woman opened her box and admired her scarf, I could see the sea of colors fill the room. Then the women put their scarves around their necks in various ways, knotted, tied, or flowing from their shoulders. I fought back tears as I hoped that Rebecca was now enjoying this scene of delight and appreciation of her handiwork, as well as the connection to God through her symbolic designs. I could hardly wait to report back to her husband, Karl, what the Holy Spirit had done with the scarves.

Again, I could not reach Karl and wondered if he was back in the hospital. After searching Facebook and calling several of his past phone numbers without response, I cryptically googled his name with the word "obituary." There was his photo and obituary. Karl had died the month before the retreat. He was found by a neighbor and rushed to the hospital, where he passed away, now with his lovely Rebecca.

After the retreat, one of the women picked up the bolts of material to be used for her high school musicals. I reserved several bolts of silk and the rest of the scarves to use for future spiritual events, not that I know when or where, just that I know Rebecca's gifts will continue to bless others. After two years in a dormant state in her closets, long after her body stopped inventing and creating, Rebecca's beautiful creations had found purpose in a way that no one could have expected. That is the amazing nature of our Creator, whose work is never done, and long after our bodies are gone from this earth, our lives will continue to tell our story.

You don't need a beautiful scarf to feel specially made or created. You can just read the account of creation in Genesis and wrap yourself up in the beautiful story of how you were made in love to love.

Session Two: The Suitcase

It was just a suitcase, the oldest looking suitcase that I have ever seen. No wheels, no fancy hardware. Just a dirty old suitcase covered in deteriorating leather, some of which had already been peeled or fallen off from use or old age. It sat in the garage of my longtime friend, Debbie, who was having a garage sale before she sold the house and left town to live near her grandkids. The suitcase did not have a price tag. It was one of the few items remaining, and I had come to pick up some giveaway furniture and sports equipment for my grandkids. I had already packed up my new old things and was saying my goodbyes to Debbie, but my attention went back to the suitcase.

"Whose is that?" I asked. It had belonged to Mindy, who had recently passed away. Debbie said, "Mindy used it for children's dramas, but recently my daughter-in-law used it as a prop for her photography. She doesn't want it; you can have it, if you want it."

With no idea in mind of how I might use the antique case, I accepted the offer and tossed the suitcase in my truck and left.

The suitcase was too dirty to take into the house, so I set it in the garage and wondered if I might use it for a skit or an object lesson in the future, or maybe just toss it in the trash. Then I forgot about it for over a year.

When I was planning the women's retreat, I thought of the session about Jesus Christ, our Redeemer, and how we not only need to accept forgiveness for our sins, but also we need to let go of any shame or guilt that we carry with those sins. God forgives us and forgets our sins, so it says in the Bible (reference), but many times we burdened ourselves with regrets and obsessing over our weaknesses. I thought of "carrying" and remembered that old leathered and weathered suitcase in the garage. I would fill it with wads of paper printed with the words of things needed to be tossed, to be forgotten, to be a part of our past but not our present nor our future: I printed each word on a separate paper and wadded it up for the suitcase, words like "shame, guilt, depression, regret, dysfunction, trauma, bitterness, perfectionism, workaholic, addiction, alcoholism, anger, etc.

When I retrieved the suitcase, I found it filled with baby blankets and onesies. After a quick check to see if my friend wanted these things, I was given permission to discard them, so I laundered them and donated them to our church's daycare. I refilled the suitcase with all the wadded up paper, all the concepts and realities and emotions that keep us from growing in our mature, spiritually fulfilled lives. I snapped the two latches to lock them in the case and loaded it into a plastic tub ready for transport to the retreat. I realized how heavy the suitcase was, even though it was just filled with 20 or 30 papers. I felt the heaviness of the burdens within and prayed that this object lesson would resonate with the women at the retreat. I also felt the heaviness of some who were coming, even though I did not know any specifics of their circumstances. It was also an exercise for me, to remind myself that I have become a new creation through Jesus Christ and that my past weaknesses and poor decisions do not define who I am today. If I dwell too much on my former self, I start to feel dragged down and dragged back to the past loaded with poor decisions. Consciously, I recall the good times of my past and recite my favorite scriptures that encourage me to press forward with the Lord. I thank God for forming me and reforming me to a better version of my younger self. I am thankful for the chance to help others let go of anything keeping them from maturing in Christ. What I didn't expect is how God was to use the old leather suitcase in a more meaningful way.

During session 2 about Jesus and forgiveness, I had planned to lug the suitcase into the room, talk about what we drag around that can weigh us down and how we can let Jesus help us to relieve us of our burdens. I was going to unwrap each ball of paper and announce what might be an issue for any one of us. I had planned to wear a lapel microphone, but it was not functional that weekend, so I only had the use of a handheld mic. Even though I was annoyed by the change, this caused me to ask the women in the room to help me. What happened next can only be described as a "God thing."

The first woman unwrapped the word "perfectionism" and announced, "Nailed it! That's me!" The next woman read "workaholic" and said, "How did you know?" Another read "depression" and said, "I'm working on it." One by one, the faces and voices made it clear that the Holy Spirit was connecting each woman with an issue specific to her. Then in a spontaneous move, a young woman came to me with a determined look and bright eyes, speaking into the microphone, "I haven't seen mine yet: trauma!" and returned to her seat. I can still see the urgent expression on her face and prayed for her that night. Weeks later I had learned that she had been trying to mask her feelings and guard her comments at her table just to "get through the weekend" when she was "compelled by the Lord" to get up and share publicly what had a private hold on her. It was after she got home when she let the tears flow until there were no more left. The shared experience of the retreat helped her to open her heart for cleansing and relying on God to help her to get to a better place spiritually and emotionally.

Around the tables women had shared their responses to the suitcase experience. They had connected to the lesson in a deeply personal way, and I thanked God for using the object lesson to tap into our emotions and reliance on the Lord to help us in our specific circumstances.

Later I called my friend and told her that God had used that old suitcase in an amazing way. I was curious about the history of the suitcase and learned that it had belonged to Mindy's grandmother. Mindy kept it as a sentimental reminder of her grandmother, for it was Mindy and my friend Debbie who had led Mindy's grandmother and close friend to accept Jesus as their Lord and Savior when they were well into their 80's. Of all the journeys in her grandmother's life, the journey to the cross and to heaven was the most precious of all. The old leather suitcase was a sweet reminder of what we can't take with us and what we can take into eternity: a life with Jesus.

I also learned that Debbie had led Mindy to work in children's ministry with her, where they had been active for many years before Mindy's death. Mindy had also become a favorite spiritually aunt to Debbie's children. Together the two were a force for Jesus in the inner city church.

Of course, now the suitcase has become sentimental to me as a reminder of God's transformative work in our lives. The dirty, peeling, leathered suitcase is out of the garage and in our home in a large plastic tub for safe keeping, for Who knows when or how it will be used again to transform lives in the future?

Session Three: Dot-to-Dot

For a long time, I have tried to describe how the Holy Spirit works in my life. I have never been gifted with speaking in tongues, nor have I fallen out on the floor of a church service. My spiritual connection with God comes more through the gift of tears, lots of tears. When the tears flow or the voice catches in the throat from being overwhelmed by God, I know that the Holy Spirit is at work. When I see visions in my mind's eye as I swim in the mornings and pray, I cannot explain how this happens, just that it does. How was I to describe the Holy Spirit at work in the women's retreat? A prophetess had already prayed over me before the retreat and told me to be ready to communicate through my tears and to keep on speaking through them, because there would be many tears flowing at this retreat. To help me, I tapped my mentee, Francesca King, to speak about Jesus, to sing her original songs, and to communicate when I would be at my weakest moments. God had a way of connecting me with other women who could fill in the gaps, and this is where I found the lesson on the Holy Spirit. It is the Holy Spirit who "connects the dots" for us, who connects ideas, people, the Living Word of Scripture, praise,and prayer to move in and through us. Dot to dot, starting with step one: in the beginning was the Word, then came prayer as talking with God, then praise and worship, then the community of believers. That was it! That's how I think of God the Creator, Jesus the Redeemer, and the Holy Spirit the Guide all connected in the Trinity in my life.

To demonstrate this concept, I purchased books of dot-to-dot inspirational and Christian images with 500-1,000 dots on one side of the page and reflective questions and Scripture on the back as an example of how we connect with God. We start with step (or dot) number one: the Word of God. As we learn about God, we move to step two, then three, etc. If we find ourselves misdirected or misguided, we erase our incorrect path and find our way again. As we connect more and more dots, we discover the "big picture" of God, how God works, how God uses us to lead others to Jesus, and how we gain more wisdom as we connect with a community of believers in prayer, praise, worship, and studies together. Talking, sharing, writing, singing, walking, praying, listening, showing compassion and understanding, and all the things that happen when God's people (in this case, women of God) gather together for the purpose of growing closer to each other and closer to the Lord.

The Holy Spirit was visible in big and small ways. When the committee arrived to decorate for the event, the turquoise colored conference chairs exactly matched the teal and purple centerpieces and table cloths brought from home.

When our group sang praise songs, the conference coordinator had asked us to keep the volume to a minimum because of a group meeting in the next room. After our first session, we were asked by the group next door to sing louder because they were enjoying our music so much. The Holy Spirit not only filled our room, but the room next door! Some songs had accompaniment, and some were sung acapella, but the combined voices in the room sounded like a choir of angels with beautiful harmonies, tones, and emotion that I rarely hear outside of a church choir. One woman filmed the singing, and I have played it over and over, remembering these precious moments in praise.

Session Four: Prayer Walk, Crafts, and Testimonies

At the retreat, women were given options in the middle of the day to take a prayer walk, to make a craft, to eat lunch, and to spend time sharing. For their prayer walk guided by a booklet of reflective questions and scriptures, some women walked through the woods of the state park, some sat by the lake and prayed, and others sat at tables in the sun outside on the patio. For the craft, Scrabble letters were available on a table with picture frames and stickers for women to choose specific meaningful words, such as "Imagine", "holy", or "word" to feature in their designs. For many, this hands-on activity brought peace and focus with time for quiet chatter around the table. At lunch time, women shared time with old and new friends, laughing and chatting at tables inside and outside. The images of women gathered together with purpose and personal sharing reminded me of accounts in the Bible where God walked with Adam and Eve through the Garden, through nature, and spoke with them; where the chosen people gathered around the table in their homes and gave thanks to God; where people gathered from all parts of the world to come to the hillsides and seasides to hear Jesus speak and teach; and where the disciples were waiting in the room to receive the Holy Spirit. God has always been in the process of gathering people closer to Him. Jesus came to gather his own to him, and in his metaphor, to gather the harvest. The Holy Spirit came to the disciples gathered together in one room and gave them the languages and the courage to spread the Gospel to all nations. That's what we do. We gather.

For the women who chose to come to a gathering of other women around the table, in nature, and away from home to focus on spiritual growth in a community of believers, this experience was so like others, yet so unlike any other. Because of the power of sharing, we offered each woman an opportunity to tell her story. In this book, we have gathered a few testimonies of what happens when women gather.

The Prayer Circle

Because prayer is such an important part of community, healing, communication with God, and expressing ourselves in silent and vocal ways, I had asked the planning committee for a circle of chairs in the back of the conference room where women could come to pray and ask for others to join them in prayer. Showing their priority on prayer as well, the committee had two circles of 6 covered chairs arranged in different corners of the room. I called on my own prayer partners, Apostle Stacie Johnson and Francesca King, to stay close to the circle during free times to be available.

Women came to ask for physical healing, and God answered our prayers. Women came asking for support and encouragement with family issues, and God gave us confidence and hope. Women came with fears, and God gave us peace. By the last session, the group of praying women numbered more than 6 as we stood together with arms around each other or hands grasped tightly. We felt the Holy Spirit so strongly as Stacie voiced our concerns and the rest of us consented with an "Amen" or "Yes, Lord" or quiet tears streaming down our faces. The rest of the room melted away, and there remained a circle of solidarity: praying women with our entire focus on God as our Healer, Provider, Hope, and Salvation. Truly we could say that the Holy Spirit was in this place, and we were happy to take that Spirit home with us.

Testimonies of the Participants of the Dayspring Women's Retreat 2022

Cindy Speakman
Director of Women's Ministry

My name is Cindy, and I am the director of women's ministry for Dayspring Church of God. In that role, I was on a committee to plan for a retreat in October, 2022. We decided to engage Nancy Hulshult for our speaker since she was also a member of our congregation. After some discussion with the team and Nancy, we decided on the theme of Imagine You!

I had several conversations and emails with Nancy during the planning process. She told me that she wanted the names of all the women registered. She was going to pull one or two each day and ask God for a Scripture for that woman and pray for her.

Early in September, Nancy and I went to the Kentucky state park where we were going to have our retreat to check out the room and equipment. As I got in the car, she informed me that on that day, my name was one that she had pulled and prayed for. We had a great time getting to know each other better and being fully prepared for the retreat.

A few weeks later in early October, my father-in-law became ill and then passed away two weeks later. Our family, including my two grandchildren who were nine and eleven, attended the funeral on a Saturday, one week before the retreat.

The following day, Sunday, my daughter-in-law, Kristie, called and asked if I could come up to Columbus to help with the kids so she could go home where her 100-year-old grandmother had taken a turn for the worse. Of course, I went up that day. Now Kristie LOVES Halloween and has many decorations around her house. I wasn't prepared for a book about witchcraft in her bedroom where I was staying.

Great-grandma passed away the next night. My grandchildren were extremely upset. She lived with her daughter, their grandmother, so they saw her very often and had a strong relationship with her. I spent some time with each child, but my grandson, Hendrix, was very upset. These poor kids had just been to a funeral for a great-grandfather, and days later their great-grandmother died as well. Hendrix went into his closet and was saying some very disturbing things about wishing he had never been born and his parents were happier before he was born. It broke my heart. Crying with him and holding his hand, I told him that I loved him, and God loved him and he wasn't a mistake. He wanted to know how I knew and I told him that it was in the Bible and I knew in my heart. He eventually calmed down.

The next day, the kids went to school and I needed to get home to do last minute preparations for the retreat. But I needed to do something. So, I went around to each bedroom and pillow and laid my hands on the pillow and bed and prayed Romans 8:35, 37–39:

"Who shall separate us from the love of Christ? Shall trouble or hardship or persecution or famine or nakedness or danger or sword? ... No, in all these things we are more than conquerors through him who loved us. For I am convinced that neither death nor life, neither angels nor demons, neither the present nor the future, nor any powers, neither height nor depth, nor anything else in all creation will be able to separate us from the love of God that is in Christ Jesus our Lord."

During the retreat, we had wonderful worship, teaching and fellowship. On Saturday, near the end of the retreat schedule, Nancy shared with everyone about her drawing names and asking God to reveal a Scripture for that woman and pray for her. She passed out scrolls that had the date she prayed and the Scripture that God had revealed to her. All around the room, people read passages with understanding and tears. My scripture, that God had revealed to her in early September, was Romans 8:35–39!

Kamille Dawkins Dungan

I Lift My Voice

*F*rom the time I was three until the time I was nine, I went through something no child should go through. My innocence was stolen from me and so was a big part of my childhood. When I was in middle school, I started to realize that dysfunction runs rampant in my family. It is crazy how the way someone breathes can cause you to run to the next aisle in the grocery store. Or how the familiar smell of a homemade cigarette can make your heart skip a beat. You want to know what is crazier though? The fact that God can redeem you from all of the craziness and trauma that you have been through in life.

Growing up and going through high school, so many things were just messed up. Between family members, friend groups, choir directors, and some of my very own decisions, I always say that I have had a good example of what not to be.

All throughout my life, I have loved to sing. I have sung at weddings, a funeral, and even at The Grand Ole Opry. I remember singing out "Strawberry Wine" and "Chicken Noodle Soup" word for word at just four years old. Two very different songs, I know. In second grade I joined the school's choir and did not stop there. When I got into high school, I finally made it into the show choir and did that freshman to junior year. I had a couple of solos and even won the title of "Best Soloist" in the unisex division at a competition. I loved singing in the show choir. What I did not love was the toxic environment that came with it: the cattiness, the smoking pot, fake friends, and a director that made poor choices right in front of me. All of it was so toxic. When the pandemic hit and everything shut down, I began working two jobs. Life was so busy. All of the built up trauma from my childhood and toxicity from high school made me shut music out of my life. I was done with it.

My husband, Ethan, and I started dating just a few months before the world shut down. We met while working at a chain pizza restaurant in our hometown. Two months before we started dating on his first day of the job and my second day, I tapped his shoulder and asked, "Hey, can you get those pizza racks off the shelf for me?"

He helped me, and my heart began to melt. Mind you, we were both dating other people at the time. Ethan told me that he had a better beard than my boyfriend's and that he did not think his relationship was going anywhere with his girlfriend.

A couple months and a couple breakups later, we started hanging out and straight away he said, "I am saving myself for marriage." I was a little nervous. I did not know what to say. Not very many people I knew had saved themselves for marriage. When he said that though, I knew he was serious. He was the first guy to want me for something other than my body.

A few days later I went to church and had breakfast with his family. When I left the table to go to the restroom, his dad asked him if we were official. Ethan told him no, to which his dad replied, "That's dumb." The next day Ethan asked me to be his girlfriend, and here we are three years later, married and living in our first home together with two awesome dogs. To this day the way Ethan looks at me with those big brown eyes makes my heart skip a beat.

When I first met Ethan's family, it was like a whole new world to me. They honor God inside and outside of church. I grew up going to church, but as soon as we got in the car after service, all hell broke loose, every Sunday. I had never seen such a good family until I met the Dungans. When I met them and got to know them, I knew my life had changed for the better. I knew I would be okay someday.

With getting to know Ethan's family, I began to grow very close to his mom, Leslie. Leslie is an angel of a woman and would do anything to help out her employees, families in her care, and her own family. She gave me a job at her childcare center when the pandemic struck. I have learned a lot of valuable things from Leslie and really look up to her. Ethan's dad, Greg, baptized Ethan and me at the end of summer in 2021. Everything we do is a family affair. I even lived with Ethan's family for eight months before we got married. Ethan so graciously gave up his room to me and stayed somewhere else so there would be no temptation. They have really shown me what true love feels like and what a true family looks like.

Over the summer of 2022 a lot of my family trauma resurfaced, and a lot of boundaries have had to be set in stone. This was and is so incredibly difficult for me. A lot of memories kept coming up in my mind and would play over and over again. It was a nightmare. Eventually, after I had talked things over with Ethan, I went to Leslie to seek counsel. I was struggling really badly. With work, family, and giving my all towards my marriage, I needed help. Leslie was there for me and found a women's ministry that does peer counseling based out of Cincinnati. I was so nervous. I had never done anything like this, but boy, was I glad I gave it a chance. I went through a big healing process by sticking with this counseling. I finished my ten sessions in November of 2022.

In the spring of 2022, Leslie told me about a women's retreat that Nancy Hulshult where would be speaking. I had never been to a women's retreat and had no idea what I would be getting into, but I love Nancy, so I thought I would give it a try. The retreat happened in October of 2022. Going into it, I was hoping that it would help me with my healing journey. It definitely did. At the retreat, our time of worship gave me chills. It made me want to use my voice again.

One of the activities at the retreat was a prayer walk. We were to walk on the trails or somewhere in the state park and find time to be alone with God. I feel like I never say the things I need to say to God, but I know He can hear me. Instead of a prayer walk, I had a "prayer sit" by the pond. I love water. I knew that if I could hear the wind hit the water and see the autumn leaves in the distance, I would be able to admire God's beautiful creation. I could just sit there and connect with Him. In the prayer guide I chose a prompt about anxiety and fear with the scripture "**Be still and know that I am God.**" Psalm 46:10 (NIV) The prayer guide suggested that I set a timer for five minutes and pray and have time with the Lord. I thought that was going to be the longest five minutes of my life, but once I started talking to God, the timer went off in what felt like a second. I could not stop. I had to keep talking with the Lord. It was as though years of childhood trauma was being released from my heavy heart. I knew God was hearing me and that He was and is with me every step of the way.

Nancy had written "imagine" on rocks and had given one to each of the fifty women attending the retreat.. She suggested throwing them out during our personal prayer time as a way to release past obstacles, whatever they may be. When I threw my rock into the pond, I could feel God's hands on me. I was okay.

During the last session of the retreat, Nancy gave each of us women a scroll of dried floral parchment paper. In each scroll was a Bible verse that was chosen for each woman during her prayer time weeks before the retreat. The verse that I received was "**Now I commit you to God and to the word of his grace, which can build you up and give you an inheritance among all those who are sanctified.**" Acts 20:32 (NIV) I did not understand it completely when I first got it, so I started looking through my Bible trying to see if any cross references made sense to me. I looked over and saw Leslie reading hers with tears falling down her face. We then shared our verses with each other.. I went first and then Leslie went. Leslie's verses were Acts 20:28-33. I heard her say, "Acts chapter 20" and thought how neat it was that we coincidentally got the same chapter. It turned out that my verse was embedded into Leslie's. I could not believe it. Leslie showed me a text that she had received from Nancy at the beginning of September. In the text Nancy explained the process of picking the verses for each woman. She explained that once she got to my verse and drew my name she thought it was too heavy for me. The next day the verse that spoke to Nancy had mine included in it. The name she had picked out next was Leslie's. How incredible is that? It was not a coincidence at all, God knew exactly what He was doing. God knew that Acts 20:28-33 would help me realize that Leslie is in my life to help me make my way through the storm and overcome the "savage wolves."

Going to this retreat and getting my verses made me realize that the thing I was after was peace. Throughout the weekend I would choose the word "peace" but the word "grace" was constantly on my mind. I kept wondering why. I then discovered that in order to get the peace I was after, I first needed to understand God's amazing grace. Then I started a whole new journey trying to understand grace. I went into this retreat as a woman who could not find her voice and who could not understand God's complete glory. I came out of the retreat a completely different woman seeking to know more about grace. I searched and I read multiple scriptures about grace, and the one I connected with the most was from 2 Corinthians 12:9 (NIV) "*My grace is sufficient for you, for my power is made perfect in weakness. Therefore I will boast all the more gladly about my weaknesses, so that Christ's power may rest on me.*" Before, I did not understand how someone could love me so much and grant me so much grace. Because I had so much to overcome, I did not realize that Christ's power is made perfect through all of my weaknesses. Now with Christ's power resting on me, I cannot stop worshiping and praising God.

I went to a Christian concert about a month after the retreat, and the opening band sang one of their original songs that I did not know. At the end of their song, they added the lyrics, "I love you, Lord, and I lift my voice to worship You, Oh, my soul, rejoice!" This was the same song that had given me the chills and had made me want to sing again at the retreat. I felt seen and heard by the Lord.

While continuing on with my walk with Jesus Christ and trying to find my voice, my husband and I started attending a very small church part time. We met with Pastor Ben and his wife, Jessica, for dinner and got to know each other better. A few weeks later Ethan and I met with Pastor Ben again for breakfast. At breakfast, Pastor

Ben asked Ethan and me what gifts we feel that the Lord has blessed us with. Ethan gave me a nudge and said, "Aren't you going to tell him?" I told Pastor Ben that I used to sing and really love it. For the rest of the day, I could not stop thinking about it. Later Ethan and I prayed about it. Was this where I was supposed to be worshiping? I had no clue. The next day at church I was so nervous and jittery. Ethan kept asking me if I was okay. I was terrified. I had never sung at church before. That afternoon I got the courage to ask what the process would be if I wanted to sing with the worship team some day. I got the information and prayed about it for the week.

The following weekend I practiced and was trying to get ready to sing in front of people again. I was terrified. When we arrived at the church I could not get out of the car. Ethan came over to my side of the car and had to practically drag me out. I had not sung publicly in almost three years! I walked into the church and got on the stage. They placed me right in the middle of the stage. I thought I would cry. Before the service, we practiced the first song, "God I Look to You." We sounded a little rough, but we got through, and it was even suggested that I lead the song. We moved on to the second song, "In Christ Alone," and my nerves started to fade away. I lead that song as well. We moved through the time of worship, and service went beautifully. After worship, I walked back to my seat, and with each step, I could feel the chains breaking and leaving my body. I had found my voice again. I had found joy in worship again! I was using it in the best way possible. I was singing to the Lord, and I could feel Him smiling at me. I am proud to be His daughter, and I will continue to sing my praises to the one True King!

As a daughter of the King, I am learning to function in healthier ways in my role as daughter and granddaughter in my family. I am learning that forgiveness and healing is a process. By dying for our sins, Jesus offers everyone redemption, freedom, and restoration from our past, not just for me but for my whole family. "*In him we have redemption through his blood, the forgiveness of sins, in accordance with the riches of God's grace.*" Ephesians 1:7 (NIV) We have new life in Him, and that is why I sing!

Stacie L. Johnson

*S*itting around the table with the ladies at the "Imagine You" retreat sparked a newness of healing and deliverance in my heart that I will never forget. It started with my friend Nancy inviting me to the retreat that she was attending, and she just happened to be the guest speaker. Well, I could not pass up this opportunity to see my friend come forth and let her light shine. Nancy sure loves some Jesus, and so do I, so this made attending the retreat a Holy Ghost invitation. I know the heart she has for hurting women and seeing them set free and delivered, so I made it my business to attend. Initially, I thought that I was going to support my friend, but God had a much deeper plan.

You see, as the months passed leading up to the retreat, I found myself as leader/Apostle being stretched to my limit just in building a ministry. I train leaders, hold a full time job in addition to being a full time wife and facilitator for other programs I teach from time to time. I was being stretched, and it did not feel good! I was tired and worn out; I was also in the middle of my health transformation, and that whole process was weighing on me. Things in my life were changing for the good, but my mindset had to catch up with all the sudden shifts I was experiencing. That meant that I was emotional at times and felt all over the place.

When it was time to go to the retreat, I was fully ready, I had arranged for some other ladies to attend and go with me, but one thing after another was happening, and they started falling off one by one. I had to go alone, and guess what? I was ok with that. I packed my bags and off to Kentucky I went. The drive down was peaceful and very inviting, and I could feel the Holy Spirit moving as I was driving. I knew that God was up to something, I just did not know what.

Once I arrived, I checked into my room. It was nice, right in the middle of a very green and quiet park. This was exactly what I needed to rest my mind and just whoosaaa a bit before I returned back home. Later that afternoon, Nancy and her mentee knocked on my door. They were going over to the hall to see what preparations had been completed, so I hitched a ride to tag along.

We then went to the park and stood on this old bridge that had a wonderful view to the lake. We prayed and took pictures, but I could definitely feel the Holy Spirit moving when we started to pray and talk about the retreat and what Nancy had in store. I knew it was going to be spectacular! I knew that God was going to move. I just did not know how.

Previously when Nancy got the invite to present, she asked me if I would help her pray with the ladies. She told me we were going to have prayer groups for the ladies; if they wanted prayer, they could just come over and receive prayer. Nancy told me she would have the oil, and the chairs would be in a circle in order to make it more intimate. It sounded great, and I was ready for whatever God was going to do.

That evening the Day Spring Church ladies had some powerful worship, and man, could they sing praises unto God! They set the atmosphere for a powerful move of the spirit. Nancy spoke, and she did an outstanding job. When it was time to pray, I could tell that the ladies seemed a little bit apprehensive, so Nancy and I stood in the prayer circle waiting. Then a lady walked over who was dealing with a lot of depression and unforgiveness. As I began to pray for her, I could feel God releasing her from the bondage of fear, regret and unforgiveness. My friend Nancy began to give her a word from the Lord, (I call Nancy Prophetess, she knows what she is) and as she gave the words, it seemed like things were just falling off her. Well, people around heard the prayers, and we could feel the tangible anointing that moved them to come over and receive prayer.

Another young lady God had me pray for another young lady, and we could feel the Holy Spirit so strong that her mom came over and stood beside me. She said she felt the power of the Holy Spirit all over me when I was praying (Glory be to God). I can't recall what I prayed at that specific time and date, but it was powerful enough to push tears from that young lady's eyes.

Another lady God had me pray for was having some serious back issues to the point that it was hard for her to walk. As we began to pray and lay lands on her back, we called her body into proper alignment, and we spoke to that pain and for it to cease! It was powerful to see God move on his leading ladies.

Sometimes as leaders, we think that we are going for one reason, and then God shows up and does something totally different which will blow our minds. That night was awesome. That night I learned some valuable lessons, and one of them is to never settle for what's in front of you. You may be tired; you may feel you have nothing left to give, let alone to share; but if you put your trust and faith in Him, he will prove His word to you and to others. It was a powerful experience, I was thinking in the back of my mind that I had nothing left to give, that I was not feeling anything, that I was just going to go with the flow! Not so, God had a whole another plan for the retreat weekend with everyone in mind.

That night the presence of the Lord was so strong in my room that I dreamed all night long. That next morning, we had to be at the conference center early so we could get started. They had prepared breakfast for us, and it looked great. Nancy had an old suitcase, and in that suitcase all I can remember was the sheets of paper that had trauma words written on them, and these words were passed out and given to us. As she expounded on her lesson for that day, you could see God re-breaking areas of women's hearts so they could properly mend and heal.

Nancy told the story about her dad, which stirred up my hidden feeling about my dad, but I held it all in. As Nancy was getting choked up and I could see the tears in her eyes, I had to then pay attention to my own eyes, because it felt like I was being hit with a two by four right in the gut! I told my inner self that I did not come here for this, to cry all over the place and expose my feelings about my dad in whom I didn't wish to speak of openly.

After Nancy's presentation, we all sat at the tables and had some open discussion about how we were feeling and what the Holy Spirit had done for us. All of the stories were touching and very uplifting. When it became my turn to share, I started talking about my dad and how down through my childhood he was never present; he was never in that role of a father that I so desired, so we had a severe disconnect. As I got older, I was always reminded of the stories of him being an alcoholic and homeless living "from pillar to post" as the old folks used to say. We did not have a very good relationship; and I must say, after you hear the damaging stories as a child, and you see some of the behaviors match what you have been told throughout the years, it's not only damaging to the child but traumatizing.

I was that girl, who grew up always seeking love from the wrong men, looking to be loved and valued in all the wrong places because I never knew the pure love of a father, so it led me to go astray. As I sat at the table with the ladies having some open table talk, I shared how my father passed away and I was asked by the family to eulogize him. I was torn; even though he was my father, I did not know any background history or current information about this man I rarely saw. I had his last name but never really knew that much about him, just all the bad stuff I was told. I was torn, troubled, and I really did not want to do it. It was only after I prayed and sought the Lord's face that I felt comfort. I asked God what he wanted me to do. God told me to make some calls to family members who might know some details, and then do some research about him.

I started my journey of seeking information about my dad. I knew my father used to play the guitar, but I did not know the full story. As I called around, I spoke to my older cousin, who was like a brother to me. It was only then when I learned the truth about my dad, William Frank Barnes. I learned that he was a very well-known musician, who not only played the guitar, but also wrote and taught music. In fact, he had his own school right here in Cincinnati, Ohio. My father played in jazz clubs in Cincinnati and Kentucky in addition to playing the lead guitar for a well- known jazz artist. To top it all off, my father had a group called the Eschoes, who had a few albums with KING records in Cincinnati. Wow! I had no clue that this man I had heard all these terrible stories about had such a promising and fruitful life.

As my cousin went on to share the rest of his story, I was told that right after I was born, my father was working as a gas station attendant when he witnessed a lady being sexually assaulted by a serial rapist. My dad stopped this terrible offense from taking place, and in his helping this lady, he got shot in the stomach. From his act of heroism, my father endured numerous hospital stays, surgeries, and pain. He became depressed and could no longer play his music. My mother and father split up, and he lost his family. This trauma drove my father to drink. It all started to make sense!

For years I had carried the burden of thinking my father did not want me and did not love me, but the truth was he just could not cope with all the losses and pain he endured. Plus, he had an addiction to alcohol, and back in the early 60's, there was no AA group or help like they have today. My father was not a drunk; he was a hero who had been crushed and did not know how to recover! When I learned this new information, my heart was crushed because I could have loved a little better and tried a lot harder to mend things before he left this world. God allowed me not only to repent for my behavior and thoughts, but also He mended a broken area with the new understanding that, as parents, we must tell the whole story to our children and not the bad stuff and how they hurt us. Had I known, I probably would have tried to get him some help and not view him in the shadow of disgust surrounded by all the past feelings that so clouded my mind and heart from caring enough to love him as a father. I was too wounded to open myself up and let him in. Instead, God had a different plan; he allowed me to be the person to vindicate my father's name and set the record straight! Plus, God did an instant healing of my heart and mind from all the past hurts, lies, and horrible images that had been spoken over me, my father, and my bloodline.

Attending the "Imagine You" women's retreat helped me to open up and see myself in a different light, the light God has created me to shine in. During the table talk sessions, I had the opportunity to meet some wonderful, anointed women and make some lasting friendships. Thank you, Nancy, for the invite! It was so needed, and thank you for listening and seeking God's face on how to help usher women into that place of healing, wholeness and a reality of Imagining You (themselves in God). I pray that God allows you to continue to open up your doors in helping women across the globe. I love you to life.

Jessica Hulshult

*D*riving up to the retreat, I cried out to the Lord. "Have your way, Lord!!" "I know you can, Lord." He knows my prayers, He saw me, and He heard me. I had just come from Children's Hospital with our 4-year-old, Aaron. Poor guy; I got a call to come back into the house as I was pulling out of the driveway for the retreat. Aaron had split his chin and needed stitches. I sent my mom and aunt ahead of me to the retreat while I drove him to the Liberty campus to be seen. He handled it like a champ. He laid utterly still as the nurse stood above him, sewing his little chin back together. He fixed his eyes on the screen above, held by another nurse. He didn't wince or move a muscle. Once it was over, he sat up straight and posed for a goofy picture.

I took Aaron home and thought how crazy the timing of his chin splitting with my going off for the weekend retreat was. Was I supposed to stay? Was I supposed to go? Either way, I had complete peace. I knew the Lord was with me and that whatever was supposed to happen would happen. I got home, and Mark assured me that he would be okay with the boys again. He wanted me to go. As long as he was comfortable with me leaving, I decided to see what the Lord would say to me on this ladies' weekend away.

The drive was long, alone in the car. I cried out to God, pouring out my heart to Him, asking, pleading for Him to answer me, asking Him to do what He does best.

The evening session was wrapping up when I finally got to the retreat center. Ladies were gathered around tables, talking and sharing responses to the teaching. I looked around and was able to find my mom and aunt. I joined their table and listened to the conversation. Not having heard the topic, I mostly listened and let the other ladies share. I was tired. I looked around for Nancy, hoping to catch her before the night was over. She was sitting with a few other ladies off to the side.

I walked across the room to where she was sitting and waited for a moment to let her know I had finally arrived. After waiting a few minutes, I decided to walk up and say a brief hello and then head to our room for the night. She saw me come up and suggested that I join the prayer circle. I had no intention of praying or asking for prayer. I was tired and felt I had missed anything of note shared that evening. She insisted that I meet her friend, so I did. I thought, well, I can always use prayer, so why not? Her friend asked for my hands and permission to anoint me with oil. I said yes and bowed my head.

Her prayer over me, for me, was powerful. She cried out to God. She was pleading for God's blessing over me, interceding for me In prayer. She spoke of me, of my prayer life, of my life. She prayed that God would bless and answer me because He hears me, because I did not ask for myself, but He would answer me. I was moved to tears. I could not believe what I was hearing. I did not expect to hear from the Lord that night or anything that she was praying. How did she know I was praying to Him? Crying out to Him on the drive up? I had just met her. As she was praying, others gathered around. My mother and aunt had joined in. I had never heard anyone pray for me or anyone else like this before. And what she said was my answer. He heard me. I went to sleep that night deeply moved and excited for what the Lord had in store the next day.

What a joy, what a peace, to know and follow Christ. Everything changes, but not Him. This year came with many changes for our family as we moved in September from West Chester to Lebanon: a change in church bodies and a halt in our volunteer work schedule and ministering at that church. Our sons transitioned from homeschooling to a private school setting three times a week.

For the first time in nine years, I had consistent time and space to myself while our children were in school. I spent that time unpacking boxes, working on our home, and occasionally substitute teaching while also working on my Master's in Marriage and Family Therapy.

When I heard about the Dayspring women's retreat featuring my mother-in-law, Nancy Hulshult, I was thrilled. Nancy has been using her retirement to write books and host families at the Grateful Hearts Retreat Center, while also babysitting her grandchildren and ministering to many others. I immediately recognized an opportunity to support her and invited my mom and aunt. Over the years, Nancy has spent intentional time with my aunt, hiking and enjoying talking about nature and the nature of God.

Annetta Weimer

*T*his past year our church announced our women's retreat. I am a people person; I am a "Mary" personality wise, and I can't seem to get enough of being with other Christian women. My initial response was that I really wanted to go, but money was tight and the timing was not the best, so I didn't register. I began hearing people talk about it and found out that our very own Nancy Hulshult, who has several books published, was to be the speaker! I really felt like I was going to miss out on something great!

One Sunday a friend asked me if I was going. She was looking for a roommate! I don't remember if my husband was there, or if I mentioned it in passing, but Ed said, "You should go." Hallelujah! I called my friend, and we turned in our registration! I was meant to be there. Nancy, her co-author, and her publisher were all there! The theme was, "Imagine You"!

Nancy had poured her heart into preparation, evident by several things that really touched our hearts! She had taken time to pick out a scripture for each of us, which she had printed out and rolled in a scroll! Then she told us about a relative of hers that had passed away from brain cancer. Her name was Rebecca had made scarves, which her husband passed on to Nancy. As each scarf was chosen for each person, it was remarkable how everyone either had an outfit on that the scarf matched, or it was their favorite color or had a significant connection! Mine matched my outfit perfectly! I know that Rebecca and the Lord were both pleased.

Another special blessing was a group of quilters, who were in the adjacent room and were blessed by our singing! There are so many stories coming out from this retreat and many connections made. I was blessed to be able to speak to all three leaders and received contact numbers from the publisher after I shared my story. I was blessed to connect and spend time with several ladies whom I admire.

I came home motivated and encouraged! I have made some strides toward my book and have an example of what I think is close to what God gave me. It still needs work; I'm hoping my son Matt will help me. He has real artistic talent and does a lot of sketching. God always opens doors for me and for everyone who puts their trust in Him.

In closing, I must share a bit of my own testimony. I have been in church since I was 6 weeks old - every time the doors were open. This was back when revivals lasted two weeks! I accepted Jesus into my life at one of our Vacation Bible Schools. I remember it was my birthday. I'm not sure of which birthday, but it was somewhere around the age of 12. I had worn a new outfit, a matching turquoise blouse and skirt, and I felt very grown up. I had always known of God's love for me but realized I needed to make it personal and desired to know Jesus better. It took me a long time to wean off the milk of the Word and get into the meat. One of the turning points was a Bible study on the book of Philippians by Warren Weirsby. I finally understood that I did not have to accept everything that people or society said about me; I had a choice. I choose joy every day! Joy is putting Jesus first, others next and then me! No one can steal my joy unless I allow it! With the help of the Holy Spirit, I will hold fast to this truth! May the peace that passes all understanding go with you and bless those around you!